Chicken Tractor:

The Gardener's Guide to Happy Hens and Healthy Soil

by

Andy Lee

ISBN 0-9624648-2-1

The information in this book is, to the best of the publisher's knowledge, true and correct. The author and publisher have exhaustively researched all sources to ensure the accuracy and completeness of information contained within this book. However we assume no responsibility for errors, inaccuracies, omissions or any other inconsistency and cannot be held responsible for any loss or damages resulting from information contained within the book. Any slights against people, programs or organizations are unintentional.

Library of Congress Cataloging-in-Publication Data

Lee, Andrew W., 1948-
Chicken tractor : the gardener's guide to happy hens and health soil / by Andy W. Lee. --
p. cm.
Includes bibliographical references and index.
Preassigned LCCN: 92-076194
ISBN 0-9624648-2-1

1. Chickens. 2. Organic farming. 3. Sustainable Agriculture. 4. Truck farming. 5. Waste products as fertilizer. I. Title

SF487.L44 1994 636.5
QBI93-22295

Published by:

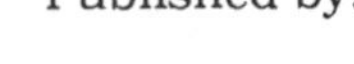

Good Earth Publications
P.O. Box 898
Shelburne, Vermont 05482
Phone and fax: 802-425-3201

Printed in the United States of America on Recycled Paper

Acknowledgments

Howard W. "Bud" Kerr, Jr.—The only person I've ever met who uses a hand-carved rooster head made from a peach branch as his calling card.

Gene Logsdon—Everybody's *Contrary Farmer.*

Phil Laughlin—Cover design, creative advice and computer wizardry.

George DeVault—For inspiration and good humored support all the way from Moscow.

Betsi Fox—For hours of literary and technical input and for rescuing a batch of chicks from the post office.

Patricia Foreman—whose input was enough to co-author this book.

Michael Fox and Melanie Adcock—United States Humane Society, for their contributions to this book and for their dedicated efforts in advocating the humane treatment of poultry and all livestock.

Donald Bixby—American Livestock Breeds Conservancy, for the service he and his organization provides in preserving our heirloom livestock.

Ron Macher and Paul Berg—For supporting small-scale farmers through their magazine *Small Farm Today,* and for their wonderfully witty and profoundly clever poem, "*Ode To A Chicken Tractor*".

...and to those trillions of chickens

who have served and befriended mankind

for the millennia.

We all owe these feathered fowl great honor

for their products and services.

Thank you chickens of the world!

About the Author

Andy Lee is co-founder and Executive Director of the Center For Self-Reliant Living and co-founder of the Ten Stones Cohousing Community in Charlotte, Vermont. He is the author of the best selling book *BACKYARD MARKET GARDENING, The Entrepreneur's Guide To Selling What You Grow*. His work has appeared in leading magazines such as *Organic Gardening*, *Country Journal*, *Newsweek* and *Vegetarian Times*.

Andy teaches permaculture, market gardening and biointensive gardening at the University of Vermont Continuing Education. He has received numerous awards, including the *Excellence In Agriculture Award* from Renew America Foundation, the 1992 U.S. Mayor's Award For *The Fight Against Hunger*, and the *Silver Spade Award* from Janus Institute.

We dedicate this book to

Richard and Marie Foreman

Ode to a Chicken Tractor

"Chicken Tractors, Chicken Tractors! I want them Everywhere!"
says Andy Lee, "I want them spreading coast to coast—LA. to Delaware."
"What this country really needs — a chicken in every pot;
and with this handy method, well, gosh, that's just what you've got!"

Stick all your chickens in a pen that you can move around;
Take them out into your fields and let them peck the ground.
It may seem silly, but it's not; the benefits abound.

They fertilize, they spread manure, they dig up all the weeds,
and they won't need as much to eat to satisfy their needs.
They're open range, but in a pen so they can't eat your seeds.

You'll make a profit, simple too, its elegant and neat;
A positive and easy way to help you grow your meat;
as a system, guaranteed, the method can't be beat.

So if you want this great technique, then this is what you do:
Buy the book by Andy Lee; it just came out - it's new.
Chicken Tractor is it's name. It's good! and useful too!

by Ron Macher and Paul Berg,

Small Farm Today Magazine

TABLE OF CONTENTS

Foreword:

Empowering The Chicken: When The Old Cocks Crow, The Young Ones Learn

by Howard W. "Bud" Kerr, Jr.

WASHINGTON DC—Growing up in America during the 40's and early 50's was certainly a lot different from today. Back then, World War II was in full swing, and people all over our country were going "all out" to win it. There were scrap drives to collect aluminum, rubber, fat and so forth. Some local folks took on the responsibility of being the Air Raid Warden or aircraft spotter, and there were Victory Gardens in practically everyone's yard.

In 1944, I was a 4-H member active in all the above; plus, I raised chickens. Fifty years ago it really was popular to have "chicken every Sunday". I grew the chickens out in our backyard. With maturity they learned to greet the morning light uttering the characteristic cry of the rooster. These raucous cries usually came from the very ones destined to become the centerpiece on our family dining room table. The pullets enjoyed a more favorable life. In time, they graduated from the light framed 12- by 6- by 3-foot chicken-wire covered frame that was their yard during their growing up and feathering out days. Daily I moved the pen around our backyard to give the chicks new turf to explore. The difficult task was moving the "home" that accompanied the moveable pen. This box was 4- by 4- by 3-feet and was both heavy and awkward to move. Regardless, this was the way I raised my 4-H project baby chicks until they were old enough to move to the hen house and begin egg production.

The livelihood of my mother's father was general farming and it must have agreed with him. He lived to 93 years of age. My mother and father's hobby farm was about 2 acres located in the suburbs of Baltimore, Maryland; however, it was country enough that there were many small family farms in our neighborhood. My mother's sister and brother each operated very large dairy farms in this same area. My mother, who lived 89 years, imparted her agrarian background into my lifestyle at a very young age, and in a number of ways, through gardening and animals, and I love the pastoral way. She gave me a favorite saying, learned from her mother, and since passed on to my children.... "As the old cocks crow the young ones learn." My method in the art of raising chickens in the back yard was taught to me by my parents who learned from their parents... "As the old cocks crow the young ones listen!"

In recent years, families—both in rural and urban environs—have begun to create special opportunities for family enjoyment, by seeking enriching activities together. Their programs are quite varied and range from journeys to distant places to "staying in our own backyard". Yesterday's "Yuppie Puppies" are now middle aged. Their lust for travel and to be the biggest has declined and for some the rungs on the ladder of success have bent or broken from the weight of stress filled responsibility. They are now content to live a more peaceful lifestyle at home with the family. Backyards are becoming again a place for pleasure, work and enjoyment. "As the old cocks crow the young ones learned".

Activities that can be shared by both parents and youngsters are not easy. However, small scale gardening and raising poultry fits right onto the large acreage lots that most municipalities now require. Makes no difference if the project is a hobby or for profit; the family will require time, learning and a sharing of the rewards. Andy Lee, in his book, *Chicken*

Tractor, has managed to combine past methods of poultry raising with today's intensive gardening techniques.

The chicken really is the tractor in today's garden. It not only enriches the soil, but also builds the soil so that gardening opportunities are maximized. At the same time, there are eggs and meat for the family to consume or sell, and even feathers for crafts. All of this leads to a fulfillment of the entrepreneurial spirit that drives the success of small-scale farmers all across this land. "As the old cocks crow the young ones listened!"

Howard W. "Bud" Kerr, Jr., Director
Office for Small-Scale Agriculture
United States Department of Agriculture

Preface:

The Second Coming of the Backyard Chicken Farmer

by Gene Logsdon

UPPER SANDUSKY, OHIO—I am always glad to see the local U. S. Commission Company sell chicks every spring at a good price to the buyer and thereby encourage more people to raise a few chickens. The company wants to create more markets for its feed and this is the right way to do it rather than encouraging huge chicken and hog factories that make more problems than they are worth.

The old-fashioned practice of raising a few chickens in the back yard or on the small farm is coming back into vogue. Chickens are easy to raise for eggs and meat, and the quality and taste of the backyard variety is superb. There are several people in our county who make a business of cleaning and dressing chickens, or you can do it yourself as we do without much fuss and bother. The fact that zoning in towns allows residents to raise a barking, crapping dog the size of a small elephant, but not four hens for a steady fresh egg supply shows just how lacking in common sense we have become as a society. The indictment against town chickens stemmed originally from roosters crowing at dawn and waking the neighbors. The easy solution to that problem is to raise only hens or butcher the roosters before they mature enough to crow all the time.

Parker Bosley, a gourmet French master chef and restaurateur in Cleveland, has often lamented to me the lack of tough old hens and roosters available to him for his famous version of coq au vin, which roughly translated means chicken stewed in wine. I told him he could have my old hens free if he returned just one as coq au vin, but I live too far away to be convenient to his purposes.

Coq au vin parties are, I hear, becoming popular amongst the yuppies. In a recent article in Ohio Week, Bosley reports that he has indeed found some small farmers in northeast Ohio who supply him with two or three year old chickens—younger ones just don't have the proper taste qualities for coq au vin. I admire Parker a lot because not only has he familiarized Ohioans with how good local food can be, but because he is not afraid to point out how Ohio State University poultry scientists have ignored small chicken farmers in favor of stinking, polluting commercial chicken factories (as long, of course, as the stinking, polluting chicken factories are not built near OSU professor's homes). In his efforts to track down or encourage producers of various good foods (he makes a great dish of guinea hen, too) he says that Ohio State "agricultural" experts have not only not been of any help, but have acted as if his requests were outlandish.

Now comes across my desk another example of innovative backyard chicken farming. Andy Lee farms in New England and writes about his outlandish farming ideas, like I do. His new book is called *Chicken Tractor.* You'll have to read it to find out what that means, but it's one heck of a good idea, and it has the potential to quadruple your garden yields in no time flat.

What I like about innovative people like backyard coq au vin producers and whacked out farm writers is that in the process of pursuing their main goal, they always seem to turn up intriguing sidebars of information. For example, Andy reports work at Ohio University in Athens, (not OSU to be sure) where scientists have increased production per foot of garden space by 700 percent in 7 years, WITHOUT any commercial fertilizer or pesticides or even petroleum powered machinery. This is a far greater increase than anything agribusiness has accomplished with all its chemicals and new iron. Remember those figures the next time you hear the mouthpieces of agribusiness trying to tell you that without pesticides millions of people will starve to death. They are starving to death NOW because they are not being taught how to quadruple their food supply with these affordable back yard methods.

Also, Lee unearthed a very intriguing bit of research. I find it hard to believe this research, but it apparently has some validity and anyway, it's the sort of thing we need to know more about. It appears that the stomata of plant leaves—that is the tiny pores through which plants can take in moisture and some nutrients—open wider than normal in reaction to pre-dawn birdsong! So an experimenter by the name of Dan Carlson played early morning birdsong tapes to his plants and found that the leaves would "*imbibe more than seven times the amount of foliar-fed nutrients and even invisible water vapor...that exists, unseen and unfelt, in the driest of climatic conditions*". Laugh if you will, but scientists in Pakistan claim that using this method has enabled them to increase potato yields 150% above national averages.

The ag economists laugh at me but I'm telling you, the dynamic future lies in the hands of backyard chicken farmers like Andy Lee and food crafts people like Parker Bosley.

Gene Logsdon
The Contrary Farmer

Introduction

It's always an interesting question as to what compels us to do the things we do in our lives. I started raising my own fruits, vegetables and livestock because I have a passion to grow things and because I like good food. I wrote this book because I yearn to share my knowledge and to become part of something bigger than myself. Something noble, fulfilling and of service to others who also seek a quality way of life in a humane environment. *Chicken Tractor* outlines my experiences and gives my opinions of the way a sustainable food supply system could be, and how a responsible poultry business should work.

I like good food and I've learned to pay particular attention to where my food comes from. For years I've noticed that much of our food no longer tastes as good as it did when I was a child. This seems to be especially true with chicken. Missing is that lip smacking, finger licking old fashioned flavor and home grown goodness of my momma's chicken dinners on Sunday.

Family farms used to grow chickens; now factory farms grow them. Huge industrial conglomerates own or control most of these factory farms. They now dominate commercial agriculture. Because of the nature of these industrial facilities, the care and feeds that are given, and the crowding in filth that occurs, commercially raised chickens no longer taste as good as they used to. Worse yet, there is a very real possibility that commercially produced poultry that you buy at the supermarket is diseased or contaminated. Some of these diseases, *salmonella* is one example, can be lethal to humans. In today's agri-industry it's very clear that we need to make a choice, and there are 2 options. We can do more of the same thing harder, or we can change.

Today we have unhappy and under-paid poultry producers, dissatisfied and malnourished consumers, and inhumane treatment of livestock and poultry animals. The final insult is a degraded environment, caused in part by the industrialization of poultry growing with its attendant wastes and pollutants. We need profound and swift change at all levels of the industry, from consumer to producer to multinational conglomerates.

Food producers can do more of the same old thing, by adding more acreage and crops and increasing livestock units. They can hope the increased volumes will produce a short-term profit and never mind the consequential hidden environmental costs and problems.

This is simply "more of the same" and it hasn't worked. We need to change. We can learn advanced and appropriate growing techniques, try new crops and different marketing strategies, and biggest of all, change our way of thinking. As a big first step in changing our attitudes about food production let us encourage food producers to think locally when they plan each year's crop and marketing strategy. Changes like this will only come about through a change of attitude and perspective.

Change is what this book is about. The meat industry has become vertically integrated. One company and its subsidiaries can control everything, including the grain fields, the breeder flocks, broiler and layer houses, and processing facilities. They claim they are doing what they have to—paying the growers far below value—to keep prices low for American consumers. Low prices, sure, but at what real cost? Contract poultry growers in this country only get about 4 cents per pound on every broiler they raise for the processors. Once they are through paying their bills these growers often have little money left to live on.

Many consumers are fed up, literally, with bland, often off-flavored poultry products. Some consumers fear poultry products laced with antibiotic and chemical residues.

So there you have it. American agriculture finds itself immersed in a rebellion. On the one hand, growers are rebelling against the high cost of confinement feeding. Consumers, on the other hand, are rebelling against the insipid flavor and low nutritional value of the product they buy. Both producers and consumers are becoming alarmed about the over-use of potentially carcinogenic chemicals in farming. We all share concern for the environment, and we all feel concerned about the inhumane treatment of animals in the meat factories.

Let's recognize our situation for what it is. It's an impending disaster that may lead to chaos in the industry and in the environment. There is an ancient Chinese aphorism that says "*where there is chaos there is opportunity!*" So, while the poultry industry is preoccupied with chaos, there is an opportunity for you, small-scale gardeners and agriculturists to get in the poultry business with little money, with limited skills and on a small piece of land.

Conventional commercial farming, especially poultry production, is a high stakes gamble in the commodities markets. If you want to be in the game it will cost you anywhere from $100,000 to $500,000 to get started. Forces beyond your control—weather, markets, feed and other production costs—are erratic and unpredictable.

Many producers report net profits in only one of three years. One good year out of three just isn't good enough. So stay out of commodities and get into farming, real farming, where farmers make a living and consumers get satisfied by the superior products and service they receive.

Chicken Tractor can give you the ideas and tools necessary for successful poultry production. However, it's up to you to learn how to use them, in your climate, on your soils and in your market place. Don't spend time arguing with me about how it won't work. Instead, spend your energy learning how to improve the system so it will excel for you.

So What is a Chicken Tractor Anyway?

Since I started writing this book two years ago the question almost everyone asks is, "*What is a Chicken Tractor, anyway?*". Sometimes I ask the questioner to give me his or her definition of the term, then chuckle at the sometimes silly answers I get.

I first heard the expression "chicken tractor" back in 1991. In that moment I instantly conjured an image of a whacked out hormone crazed rooster in a duckbill cap racing a low-rider John Deere across the landscape, banging into the barn and careening down the fencerows. Sort of a silly idea isn't it? Heck, chickens can't drive tractors. Can they?

I've never seen a chicken drive a tractor, or a bus for that matter, and I bet you never have either. I do know, though, that chickens can do many things a tractor can, some better, some worse. They can also do a whole lot of things a tractor can't do. What is true is that chickens in the right location can do more good for your garden soil—and do it better and cheaper—than any tractor.

Chickens eat bugs, weeds and grasses, spread manure wherever they walk, give meat, or eggs day after day and almost never talk back or need new tires. They can be far more beneficial to humans when combined with the portable shelter-pen that we refer to as the "tractor" part of the chicken tractor system.

The term, "chicken tractor" is just a tongue in cheek expression coined by Bill Mollison, the irascible founder of the permaculture movement that started in Australia back in the 70's. It simply means the whole idea of putting the chickens where they do the most good and where they are easiest to take care of, in the garden.

For most Americans, buying eggs or poultry at the supermarket has become a joyless, almost suspicious act. Suspicion, that is, of the potential carcinogenic chemicals used to raise commercial chickens. We've learned through countless newspaper articles not to trust the producers of our food. They use growth hormones and inhumane feeding and housing regimens. Filth and disease permeate the processing plants.

The alternative to mass produced food is to grow your own. Until now, growing your own chickens for meat and eggs has been mostly a chicken house affair. Chicken houses themselves can be a joyless scenario, too, although not always as bothersome or frightening as buying poultry from the supermarkets when we don't know where it's been.

Where is the joy when you have to carry the feed in and the manure out of that dreary little building out back called the hen house? What a waste of energy that building is. It's expensive to build, you can't move it and the ubiquitous attached run gets smelly, muddy and unsightly. Yuck, who wants to raise chickens that way? Especially when there's a simple, inexpensive portable coop that does the work for you.

Figure 1:- Typical Chicken House That Stays in the Same Place Year After Dreary Year

If you want to fertilize a field or pasture, weed and feed a garden bed, or build a raised bed garden on poor soil or clay, the chickens will do it for you. All you have to understand is how the system works, then you can engineer changes to fit your site and needs.

There is nothing fancy, newfangled, hard-to-understand or expensive about this method. You just need plain old common sense, a keen eye and an open mind. This is a system that is so simple you can build it on a Saturday morning and put it to good use that afternoon. With proper care it will last you for years to come.

Sound too good to be true? Well, read on, and find out how others have cashed in on the method. No, it's not a "get-rich-quick" scheme, but it is a "quick fix" to get good food and healthy soil. It will save you money, either by decreasing your food bill considerably, or giving you extra produce to sell. This is definitely a food production system for people on a low-budget with limited space.

Should You Have Roosters in Suburbia?

What to do about those restrictive zoning laws if they exist in your town? Try some community activism to get the law changed. Get a grant to show people in your community how they can use chickens in the chicken tractor system without the odor and flies traditionally associated with raising livestock in suburbia. I'd rather listen to my neighbor's chickens cluck than his over-powered, under-muffled riding lawnmower every Saturday morning for the whole summer.

Zoning officials are likely to leave you alone unless they get a complaint. I once knew a fellow who kept a sow with a litter of pigs in his garden shed. None of the neighbors complained and he raised 2 litters of pigs every year.

One time, for lack of a better place, I started 300 chicks in my garage and kept them there for 3 weeks until the field pens were ready. Word got out and we had many folks stop by with their kids to see the baby chickens—including our landlords. They were fascinated! They brought their grandson over regularly to see the chicks grow. No one complained. Here's the moral of this story. Go recruit your neighbors. Enlist them into the idea. Promise them a few free eggs or invite them to a community chicken BBQ.

It is not a good idea to try keeping a rooster in suburbia. Your neighbors aren't <u>that</u> fond of you. I love chickens but I once had a neighbor who inherited a rooster named Paul. I'm not even sure now what breed Paul was, sort of a calico thing, a bit shy and underweight and his left eye looked mostly to the right, but could he crow! Loud, at all hours of the day!

Do you have a crowing problem with your chickens? That's easy enough to fix. Just order all females. They don't crow. Yes, the hens dress out smaller than the cockerels, but hens are good for frying or grilling and you can keep a few of them to become egg layers.

What <u>drives</u> my enthusiasm about the chicken tractor idea? There are many reasons:

1. It's a system that provides a solution to several problems in the conventional raising of poultry. The system has <u>many</u> beneficial components. In permaculture we call this "stacking". It is a shining example of reciprocal benefits, where both the chickens and the grower benefit.

2. It's appropriately scaled, practical, and can be used for as few as 1 chicken, or as many as the grower has time and land to handle.

3. It's a way to get good nutritious food (vegetables, chickens and eggs) inexpensively. I've always felt that what this country needs is a good chicken in every pot.

4. It prepares the soil for optimal—versus maximum—yields of vegetables and small fruits.

5. It fulfills the part of me that wants to be self-reliant and semi-self sufficient.

6. It enables market gardeners and small-scale family farms to expand their menu and enhance profit-ability.

7. It is a humane way to raise poultry.

8. It will stimulate interest in the heritage poultry breeds that are good foragers.

9. Potentially, chicken tractors can have a positive global impact on how people reclaim land, produce their food and encourage local self-sufficiency.

The following table summarizes the real advantages of chicken tractors compared to raising poultry the conventional way.

Table 1: Advantages of Chicken Tractors

1. Low cost part time business with good return.
2. Low cost way to grow your own food that is healthy and nutritious and tasty.
3. A Chicken Tractor is smaller than a hen house or barn with its associated mud run, less conspicuous. Less costly and easier to construct.
4. Has other uses in off-season as storage or cold frame.
5. Can be brought directly to the garden, and fits into small sections where you need weed control and fertility.
6. Potentially pest proof.
7. Kids love to see the chickens in the chicken tractor and can safely help take care of the flock.
8. Chickens themselves are beneficial as:
   a. Manure machines for soil fertilization.
   b. Grass and weed grazers.
   c. Limited tillagers.
   d. Food producers: eggs and meat.

I've tried to contain in this little book all the philosophical, environmental and humane why-to's, combined with practical how-to's of everything you need to know to get started with a chicken tractor in your garden this year.

I've included how to have an inexpensive, easy to maintain, fun project you can do with your kids. The benefits to you will be great tasting poultry, super-rich garden soil, healthy exercise and a meaningful contribution to your annual food supply. The result is to give you a step toward self-reliance and semi-self-sufficiency, so that you can feel better about yourself and your environment and enjoy an enhanced quality of life.

Recipe for a Chicken Tractor

The following "recipe" gives you a jump start for your chicken tractor. The chicken tractor idea and approach can also apply to almost any breed of poultry (turkeys, pheasants, quail) and other small live stock (pigs, goats, rabbits).

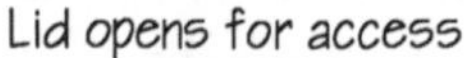

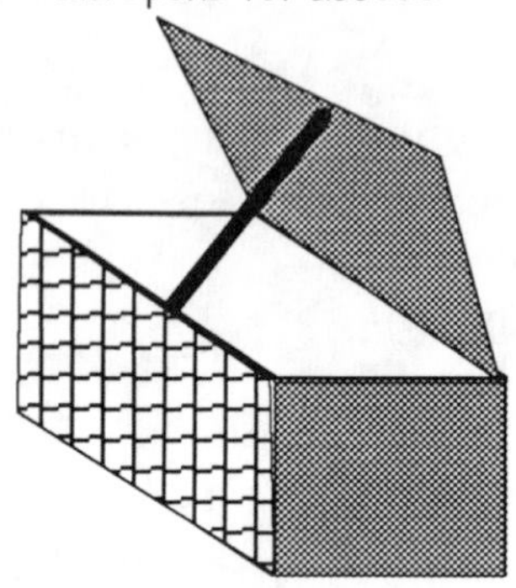

Make a bottomless, portable shelter-pen that is sized to fit over your garden bed. Install poultry wire on the top, sides and ends and cover the top and one or both ends with a tarpaulin for protection against the weather.

Add chickens: One broiler per 2 square feet, or one hen per 4 square feet.

Add fresh water and feed daily. Hang the waterer and feeder high enough to keep dirt and manure from getting in them. You can also feed vegetable wastes from your garden and kitchen scraps.

RESULT

Chickens clean your garden beds by

Eating grass, weeds and weed seeds, bugs and plant debris.

By scratching the ground (tilling).

And they add valuable fertilizer

Directly onto your garden by manuring (pooping)

THEN every day or so move your tractor to fresh graze, or add more bedding. This almost entirely eliminates the flies and smells. After the chickens have matured you can keep them for eggs or process them for a barbecue.

Chapter 1: Why Chicken Tractors Belong in Your Garden

I grew up on a rural dairy farm in southwestern Missouri where raising chickens is as much a part of daily life as waiting for the school bus and having your own dog. In those days I really didn't know too much about chickens except what my folks told me or what I learned through observation and practical application.

Like most farmers of the day, we followed the conventional pattern of growing chickens in a hen house with an attached pen. All the feed is carried in and the manure is carried out. Predators sometimes burrowed under the hen house and killed the chickens, and disease, odor and unsightliness were more common than any of us liked to acknowledge.

Forty years ago it was also common to see chicken and turkey shelters out in the fields. They were usually A-frame type buildings on skids. Losses to predators sometimes made this free range poultry business less than profitable. My parents did the same thing with A-frame pig shelters. They moved the pig shelters every so often so the hogs could root up the ground and collect acorns from the abundant oak trees that studded our 189 acre Ozark farm.

Somewhere in the back of my head was an idea for a portable chicken pen that was completely self-contained, either on skids for towing or on wheels for rolling. The chickens would be protected from predators yet still have plenty of range graze. That idea lay quietly in my inner mind for probably 30 years or better, until 3 years ago when I heard about Jerome Ostenkowski. He is a market gardener in Basalt, Colorado, who is using a "chicken tractor" to weed the beds in his garden. That's when I had a "blinding glimpse of the obvious"—often referred to as the "aha"! My interest in chicken tractors really took off, and I've been studying and practicing with them ever since.

"Chicken tractor" is more than a cute play on words. It is a practical, low-cost, no-nonsense way to raise meat and eggs while getting your garden weeded and your soil improved and fertilized. Chickens--acting as biocyclers—reduce kitchen and garden wastes to instant fertilizer as they improve the soil with the bacteria laden manure and digestive juices they excrete on the garden beds.

Obviously, you just can't let your chickens loose in the garden. They will wreck your crops in no time. That's why you need a chicken tractor. The chicken tractor is a portable, bottom-less shelter-pen for layers or broilers. It contains chickens, feeder, waterer, shade, open sunlight, protection, nest boxes and easy access for the gardener through its hinged lid.

Just move the tractor around the garden. Put it wherever you don't have food crops growing. In my garden half the beds are for the chickens, the other half for the veggies. Each year I simply rotate beds.

Now this doesn't mean I need twice as much land as a normal garden needs. What happens, instead, is that the ground becomes so fertile from the chicken rotation that I can grow twice as much food on half as much land. Using half as much land means nearly half the amount of work, too.

Moving the chicken tractor is simple. Pick up one end a few inches and drag it wherever you want it. The chickens will waddle along inside. The key to the whole thing is to make the pen light enough to move easily. During the first few moves the chickens won't want to do anything other than hunker down. There's a chance you will drag the pen over them, or at least their feet. To prevent this, just have a helper walk along behind clapping hands to chase them forward. After two or three moves the chickens will get the hang of it.

Chickens glean the beds after harvest, prepare beds for cover crops or food plants, graze paths and borders like a lawn mower, and provide an intermediate repository for garden and kitchen wastes. What I'm really doing is turning chicken into worker, grass into chicken and manure into fertilizer, all in one pass. Neat arrangement if you ask me.

Animal Tractors in Permaculture Design

In Bill Mollison's *Introduction to Permaculture* he uses the chicken to explain his Theory of Relative Location. Relative location means: place every element in relationship to others so that they assist and support each other. Buckminster Fuller called this synergy. Each component supports the entire system so the value of the individual parts is greater than the sum of all the parts, creating a more valuable whole.

Bill Mollison says it very well:

> *"The core of permaculture is design. Design is a connection between things. It's not the human, or the chicken, or the garden. It is how the human, the chicken and the garden are connected."*

This is a very thought provoking idea. It gets even more exciting when added to other permaculture concepts, such as the ones in the following chart.

Table 2: Some Permaculture Concepts*

• Each element (plant, animal, thing) has many purposes (functions) in a system.
• Each important purpose is supported by many elements.
• Emphasis is on the use of biological resources over fossil fuel resources.
• Using and accelerating natural plant succession to establish favorable sites and soils.
• Using polyculture and diversity of beneficial species for a productive, interactive system.
• Using edge and natural patterns for best effect.

* Adapted from *Introduction to Permaculture*, Page 5.

In other words it is the location of the chicken that is either very valuable or very much a problem. With chicken tractors, you feed the chicken from and in the garden, and the chicken tends the garden and feeds the human. Another term for this synergy is "stacking".

That's just what the chicken tractor does. It puts the chicken *in the right place*, in the garden. This is where its food is abundantly available and where the chicken can perform its primary functions as a meat and egg producer, biomass converter and portable manure spreader.

By having the chicken in the right location you can feed, water and care for it easily as a minor part of the daily chores of the garden. The chicken provides a handy tillage tool with its continual scratching and pecking. It becomes a biomass recycler, consuming spent garden plants, weeds, grasses, insects and excess vegetables. The manure returns to the earth as fertility for the crop. The eggs and meat nourish the gardener, while the viscera, feathers and carcass add tremendous value to the compost heaps.

Figure 2: Products and Behaviors of a Chicken

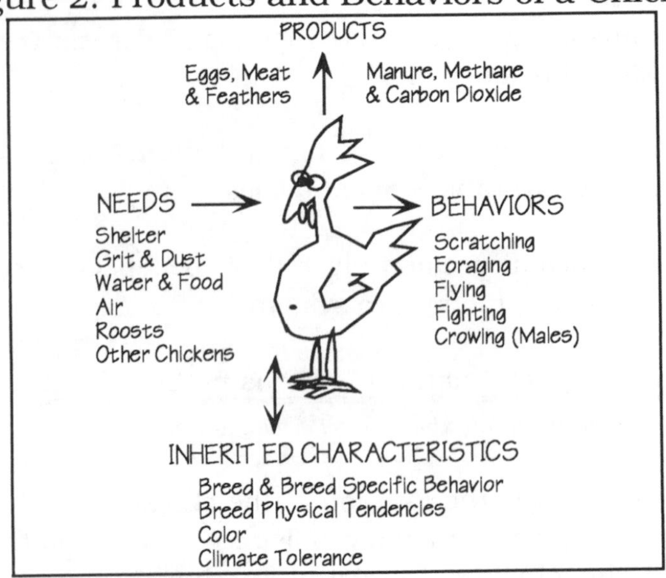

Adapted from *Introduction to Permaculture* page 6

The traditional way of raising chickens in hen houses does not view the products and behaviors of a chicken as part of a larger ecosystem. Chicken tractors bring into play the harmonious relationships with you, the gardener, the chickens and the garden.

Table 3: Functional Analysis of the Chicken

Chicken Characteristics	
Color	Size, height & weight
Heat tolerance	Cold tolerance
Flying ability	Eggs or meat
Single or dual purpose	Mothering ability
Personality	Roosting ability
Scratching & Foraging	Pecking
Inputs (Needs)	
Shelter	Air, food & water
Dust Bath	Grit
Roost & Nest area for layers	Mineral supplements
Companions - other chickens	Predator protection
Outputs (values)	
Meat & eggs	Manure
Feathers & feather meal	Heat generation
Undigested nutrients	Insect, weed & grass control
Carbon dioxide & methane	Potential pollution
Companionship, pecking & sound	Biomass converter
Scratching & tillage	Carcass/viscera
Relationships	
Food for humans	Fertilizer for the garden
Organic matter for the garden	Carbon dioxide for plants
Companionship for the gardener	Waste recycling
Soil scratching	Compost materials
Weed-disease-pest control	Meat and eggs income
Compost income	Increased garden yields
Improved plant health	Improved nutrition for the consumer

Certainly this expands our thinking to include all inputs and outputs with an eye to creating beneficial relationships and improving our garden environment. In the next section we will examine two more permaculture concepts: visible and invisible structures. These structures can either enhance or limit your ability to produce chickens in your own backyard.

Visible Structures

When you start planning your chicken tractor garden there will be visible and invisible structures that can affect your site and plan. The following section gives examples of visible structures.

- **Fences**, especially permanent fences which may be hard to move if you ever need to. These may have brushy hedgerows growing up in them that can provide food or bedding for the chickens. Maybe the hedgerow will cast a shadow, block the harsh winds or cooling summer breezes. Sometimes fencerows shelter wildlife that will stalk your chickens.

- **Roads**, especially heavily traveled ones, where the noise might bother your chickens, or the dust and fumes may cause health problems. Roads can also be our friends. They make it easy to get feed and water to our chickens, and we use them for hauling the chickens to the processing house or to market.

- **Driveways, for Access to the Chicken Tractors**. Place these in such a way as not to interfere with your chicken tractor rotation, yet close enough to deliver feed and water without undue labor. Design and build driveways for all-weather use.

- **Terrain and Slopes**, something we see every day but often fail to recognize as being important to our garden and chicken tractor layout. If the terrain is rocky or hilly it will interfere with our rotation schedule. If the land is flat, such as in a flood plain, we need to think about whether water run-off is going to present a problem for our gardens or birds.

• **Trees**, either in hedgerows or free-standing, are useful in several ways. They give us shade in the hot summer, windbreaks, lumber and posts to build our chicken tractors, and in some cases, food for the chickens. Leaves from trees are especially useful for bedding and for compost materials. Normally trees are not welcome in gardens. However, as we study the natural diversity of the landscape, we discover that trees play an incredibly valuable role in weather attenuation, landscape design and wildlife habitat, for nesting or food.

• **Houses and Other Buildings**. These can be our most important visible structures. If they are already existing it may be impossible to move them to make our rotational gardening scheme work out better. They also cast shadows, block or funnel wind and act as heat reflectors of the rays of the sun. They offer opportunities to harvest rain water for irrigating the garden or for drinking water for the livestock. We also need to consider the relative location of the household to the chickens. Nearby neighbors may not like any unsightliness or odor from your chicken pens. Always consider your neighbor's property in relation to your own when you lay out your garden plan.

• **The portable pens** themselves become visible structures. If they are in your neighbor's line of sight you want to make sure they look neat and well cared for. Think about how the pen location will affect the natural drainage of the site, and if the run-off from the pens will cause any problems in the downhill areas of your site.

Invisible Structures

It's easy to see a "visible" structure and plan how you will compensate for the influence, positive or negative, that it may have on your garden. Sometimes it's not so easy to see the invisible structures, however. These include:

- **Attitudes, yours and your neighbor's,** can have an immediate impact on your choice of a garden spot. If the neighbors don't like the idea of raising livestock for food then you have a budding quarrel on your hands if you consciously or otherwise put your chickens in their line of sight.

- **Social and cultural customs** surrounding the raising of poultry for eggs and meat in your area is certainly an invisible structure. If people in your area are receptive to a local agricultural industry you will have an easier time communicating with your neighbors about the advantages of raising poultry in this manner.

- **Zoning and Board of Health regulations** in your community can be bothersome. Many areas in this country have zoning restrictions against raising livestock. Some communities ban chickens, especially roosters. These old zoning laws are in response to odor and fly complaints and the noise pollution of roosters. If you are raising roosters for meat birds they will begin to crow strongly at least a week before they are large enough to harvest. Egg layers are much quieter of course, but you won't get fertilized eggs for hatching unless you keep one or two roosters around. To my knowledge there isn't any humane way to keep a rooster from crowing.

- **Subsurface obstacles** such as hardpan or high water table, that might cause the chickens to create boggy conditions. In this situation you can wind up with a heck of a mess if you place your chicken pens in an area that doesn't drain well. You'll get all kinds of odors and fly problems, soon followed by even bigger problems with your neighbors and your local Board of Health.

• **Prevailing winds, storms and rain**. In the Lake Champlain Valley where I live, the prevailing summer storms come out of the South. Knowing this, I always enclose the south end or side of the tractor to keep the rain off the birds. Likewise, I know that the chickens are most apt to overheat during the later part of the day when the fierce westerly sun makes its way into the pens. I can add shading to the west end of the pens to keep them cooler.

• **Climate, heat and cold**, clouds or sun, rain or dry, length of season. These all influence how successful your poultry project will be. These are things you need to know in order to plan your annual rotation of chickens. For example, you don't want to put your chickens outside until they are old enough to withstand the current weather, be it hot or cold or wet. Knowing these weather patterns will enable you to determine just how many batches of birds you can grow in any given season.

• **Disease vectors**, such as pigeons and sparrows who might come to your chicken feeders for a free meal. You want to check around your area to see if any particular poultry diseases prevail in your region.

• **Electromagnetic fields**, referred to as EMF's have a potential detrimental effect on poultry. At the moment there are conflicting reports as to whether or not EMF's cause cancer in livestock. Over the years I've heard enough anecdotal evidence to give me concern when working in areas where EMF's might exist. Personally I just don't want my birds subjected to something that is as concentrated as EMF's under a high-tension power line, or near a transformer box.

• **Natural light** is a big factor in optimal egg production, and can have some influence on how well chickens will gain weight. Putting them in a continually dark area is detrimental. Putting them in bold sunshine without some form of shade will be devastating, especially once the ambient temperature climbs over 80 degrees Fahrenheit.

• **Location of feed and water supplies** are both visible and invisible structures. If you have to truck your water from off-site you will spend much more time caring for your chickens than if your water is available from a nearby garden hose. The same thing applies to feed. If you have to truck feed from far away it can add an enormous cost to your chicken production operation. In my case I belong to a feed co-op that brings organic chicken feed all the way from mid-state New York at an added cost of .08 cents per pound. We can only buy it in 10 ton lots, so we have to have a large storage facility nearby.

• **Your overall garden plan** and your soil fertility management are important invisible structures. You need room to move the chicken tractors without encroaching on the land you need for your annual garden. Also, you don't want to apply more manure in a small space than the soil can reasonably handle.

Competing uses for the site usually come about through lack of master planning in the beginning. My first market garden in Pembroke, Massachusetts experienced this problem when my two sons decided they wanted a baseball field where my garden expansion area was. The compromise was to have my chickens moved farther back on the land, adding about 200 feet to my daily chore of caring for the chickens. Fortunately I was shrewd enough to bargain into the deal that the boys had to take over the chicken chore. Even at that the boys conned me into new ball gloves before we finished the deal.

• **Nearby processing facilities**. Being close to the slaughterhouse will help a great deal when you start harvesting your chickens. Currently I drive my broilers about 20 miles for processing, but I have friends who must drive over an hour to get to the plant. Knowing the time and distance to the slaughterhouse is critical in your planning. Transportation is a cost you need to add to your overhead, and there's always a chance not all the birds will survive a long, hot journey to the processor.

• **Supply houses for equipment, supplies and feed**. Buying supplies and equipment has become easier with the passing years as more mail order catalogs carry them. Feed is a different story, however. Long-distance trucking is costly and it's bad for the environment, even if it does employ a lot of people. If your feed transportation costs get too far out of hand you may want to start growing your own feed. This then becomes another invisible structure. Maybe it's a visible structure too, if you don't have the land to do it on.

• **Local experienced people** will often be able to help you with advice on how to get started. Many of us grew up in families where raising chickens is part of everyday life. If that's true for you then you probably know all you need to get started. Others, however, have a desire to grow chickens, but absolutely no idea how to begin. That's when friendly experienced neighbors can be invaluable. Look around your area and see who's doing it, and become friends with them. They'll probably gladly share their knowledge with you in exchange for your occasional help moving chickens or building more pens. You may be able to help start a cooperative with other small-scale growers in your area. Together you can buy bulk feed at less cost and group orders of chicks for a better price. Your group might even consider jointly buying processing or freezer storage equipment that you can share.

• **Neighborhood dogs**, even friendly, gentle ones. I learned this lesson very quickly from a 6-month old Lhaso Apso puppy named ZaZa. She is my neighbor's pet and a very playful little mop, cute as a button. Her only problem is she wants to play with the chickens. She runs along the pen yapping her fool head off and scaring the dickens out of the chickens. Hopefully we've gotten her trained out of this annoyance.

If you or your neighbor has a dog you may want to put up a fence to keep it out of the chicken area. Spend some time training the dog not to bark and chase the chickens. Dogs can also be our friends, by extending our senses far beyond our normal range. They will sense when a stranger is near, or warn us loudly when a fox or raccoon is trying to break into the chicken pen.

When you look back at the chart showing the functional analysis of the chicken tractor, you can easily understand why chickens belong in the garden. Understanding why we move the chicken tractors so frequently is a different notion. We need to rotate them daily so we can take advantage of all the benefits they offer in the garden.

Weed control, manuring, pest control, recycling waste vegetation from the garden and tilling the soil are all good reasons why we use chicken tractors. To understand this better, we need to look at some of the problems associated with stationary pens:

• **Chicken manure is potentially a hazardous waste**. When you keep chickens in just one fenced-in run, they will quickly turn it into a foul-smelling, fecal-laden spot that contains toxic levels of macro and micro nutrients, especially nitrogen. So much nitrogen will accumulate that it will turn into ammonia, killing soil life and smelling up your garden.

• **The stationary, enclosed run also becomes a site for flies**. They are always around, and the chickens eat a lot of them. However, with so much fecal matter lying on the surface the flies will get ahead of the chickens' ability to eat them. Flies will become a major nuisance.

• **In the enclosed run the chickens get dirty and don't thrive**. They need fresh pasture and fresh soil to scratch every day. If you leave them too long in the same spot you will be toxifying one garden bed while denying your other garden beds the opportunity to reap the benefits of the chicken tractor rotation.

Chickens are great biocyclers if you move them to fresh graze each day. They can get as much as 30% of their food from vegetation on the garden beds. They eat spent garden plants, weeds and cover crops, depending on where you are in your garden bed rotation. By eating fresh weeds, grasses and garden plants, your chickens will get a diverse diet, enabling them to acquire many of the nutrients and vitamins they need for vigorous growth and well being.

Get Super-Fertile Soil Fast—Using Animal Manure

For as long as anyone can remember, livestock growers have claimed extra yields from their land by applying animal manures; either raw, seasoned or composted. Most people, even many vegetarians, feel that you just can't grow good food crops without access to animal manures for fertility.

However, it's been my experience that land can just as easily be reclaimed with non-manure compost, if you have enough time and follow a good rotation schedule. Back in 1990 I helped start the Intervale Community Farm on 3 acres of worn-out corn field in Burlington, Vermont. The soil, a fine sandy loam, had about 3 percent organic matter. We had to irrigate frequently because the soil didn't hold much water, and the fertilizer requirements were almost too high to be affordable. Our yields that first year were fairly low compared to what I thought they could be.

We didn't have access to manure of any kind for making compost, so we used the next best thing, leaves and grass clippings. We worked out a deal with the Chittenden County Solid Waste District to have residents use the edge of our field as a drop-off site for leaves and grass clippings. As we had time we used the tractor to form the materials into windrows, which were turned either with a bucket-loader or a rented Wildcat compost turner.

As the compost became available we spread it on our field from 1-inch to 2-inches deep and worked it into the soil with a light rotary tilling. This practice has continued for 5 years, and the result is that the organic matter in the best parts of the field is now approaching 6 percent. The vegetable yields have improved dramatically, with the best tomato plants yielding about 3 pounds per square foot.

However, it's far more likely that yields in the 3 pounds per square foot range will come much quicker with the use of animal manure. This is especially true if the land you are undertaking to garden or farm is not very fertile to begin with. Almost always, what poor soil needs more of is organic matter. A good grade of compost that contains animal manure will usually be superior to a compost made without animal manure.

In the chicken tractor garden—with the portable pens rotating over the beds even for a few days each year—the accumulation of manure can add superb richness to the soil. With super rich soil you can expect super high yields. Of course, the other elements in the system are equally important, such as plenty of sunlight and water. You can develop a well-structured soil by sub-soiling or double-digging. The most important ingredient, of course, is plenty of intelligent management by the gardener.

Does animal manure help you reclaim and fertilize land faster? Yes! The Intervale Community Farm yields improved dramatically in five years because we were using compost, even though the compost didn't have animal manure in it. Now, here's an example of how I used compost made with animal manure to develop a super rich soil in just two years.

When I started my one-acre market garden in Pembroke, Massachusetts, back in 1979, my tomatoes yielded less than one pound per plant. Fortunately I lived near a goat breeding farm managed by Heifer Project International that had an abundance of well-aged goat manure, free for the hauling. I hauled the manure to my garden in a borrowed dump truck and spread it about 4 inches thick and then mixed it in the soil with a rented rotary tiller.

About two weeks later I put in my tomato transplants with a side-dressing of organic fertilizer. That year I had an astounding increase in yields of rich, red tomatoes, with some plants producing up to 7 pounds each! The average for the harvest was about 5 pounds per plant. The following year, after a second application of well-aged goat manure, I had some tomato plants that produced 20 pounds each, and the garden average was 14 pounds. Manure made it possible to achieve this increase in yields. My tomato harvest went from 2 pounds per plant to 14 pounds per plant (700%) in only 2 years.

As a symbol of fertility in the garden, the earthworm is a great barometer. The earthworm count in my garden went from almost zero in 1979 to over 10 worms per cubic foot in 1981, and kept climbing each year after that. I'll bet today if you dug up that soil you'd find over 1,000 worms per cubic meter. It's easy for me to see from this experience how very, very important animal manures are when used properly in a soil management program.

Chapter 2: Chicken Tractor Systems

In chapter 1 we looked at the characteristics of portable shelter-pens and some of the permaculture philosophy behind them. Now let's look at various ways to design and use the chicken tractor. It is easier to understand how the system functions if we know what we <u>need</u> from the system. In poultry production we humans need to receive food. The chickens need protection from the heat, cold, rain, sun, and predators, and they need feed and water regularly.

Traditionally, growers have used a widely varying array of hen or broiler houses—often with attached wire-covered runs. The problems with such a set-up are numerous. We carry the feed in and carry the manure out. Diseases and parasites build up in the building and in the enclosed mud run. The chickens don't have access to clean soil or fresh graze. Of course, if you want to, you can spend time and energy cutting weeds or grasses and bringing it to them.

Much of the manure, especially what is in the enclosed run, is not recoverable. Nutrients volatize or leach away quickly. The soil becomes over loaded with toxic levels of nitrogen, phosphorus and potassium. Unless you clean the enclosed run regularly, it becomes unsightly, odiferous and offensive after only a few days or weeks.

The "tractor" part of chicken raising is the best overall solution to these problems. This is not a new idea. The only thing new is the creation and refinement of an integrated system. There are 7 basic chicken tractor models with variations on a theme with each one. The table below summarizes the systems. We discuss each of these systems in the following section.

Table 4: Chicken Tractor Systems

System	Characteristics	Comments
1. Rotational Garden	Uses bottomless shelter-pen that you move daily in the garden .	Need room to move pens around garden.
2. Deep Mulch System	Stationary bottomless shelter-pen. Add fresh bedding daily.	Creates a raised garden bed.
3. Sheet Mulch System	Bottomless cage that stays on garden beds longer than 1 day, but shorter than life of chickens.	Puts a sheet-mulch on top of beds.
4. Intensive Grazing in Paddocks	Have a fixed or movable hen house and rotate grazing in paddocks. Egg mobiles are a good example.	Must clean hen house regularly but still gets most of the manure on garden. Good for layers.
5. Polyface System	Mixes species, e.g., chickens follow cattle in field. Good application for egg mobiles	Great parasite control.
6. Hens on wheels	The hen house is mounted on wheels for easy moving around the garden	More costly to build and harder to keep clean and maintained
7. Greenhouse Systems	Creates eco-system, balances oxygen from plants and carbon dioxide from chickens	Can protect chickens through winter season.

1. Rotational Garden System

The basic rotational garden system is simply to house the chickens in bottomless, portable shelter-pens that are the same width of your garden beds. You can choose whatever length you want. When the garden bed is not producing crops you put a chicken tractor on top and let the chickens glean, till and fertilize the bed for the following crop.

Figure 3: Rotational Garden System

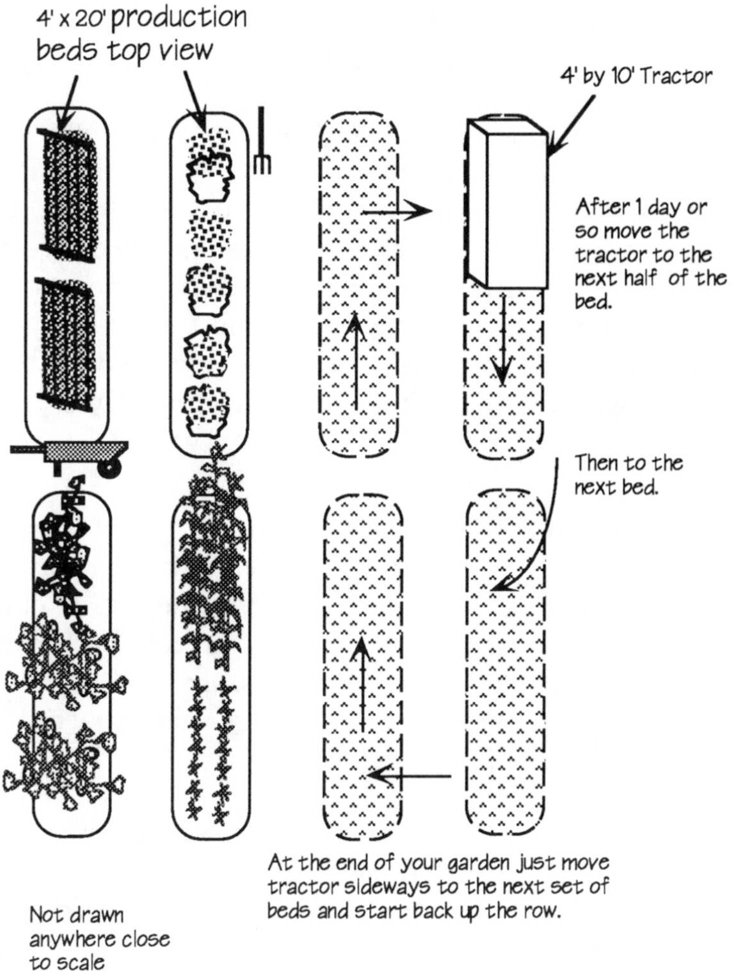

My garden is twice as large as it needs to be for food production alone. This enables me to rotate and improve each garden bed every other year as shown by the figure above.

My garden beds are 4- by 20-feet. That is too long for a structurally stable pen. I use a 4- by 10-foot pen and move it from one end of the bed to the other. Once the entire length of the bed has been "treated", I move the pen across the path to the next bed. I repeat this pattern, treating all the beds until the birds are ready to harvest.

In really hot weather, above 90 degrees F, use extra shading material for the chickens. If you see them panting they are too hot, and will sometimes die from suffocation if you can't cool them quickly. To cool the chickens, place wet burlap bags over the pen. Any slight breeze moving through the wet burlap will move the moisture and drop the air temperature by as much as 10 degrees F. In really cold weather wrap an extra tarp over the pen to keep the chickens from chilling.

2. Deep Mulch System

In some gardens there simply isn't enough room to move the chicken tractor to a new piece of ground each day. Other times the soil is so infertile, rocky or filled with clay that nothing will grow in it. In these instances you can use the deep mulch system to create incredibly rich garden beds above the surface. With this method you never need to rotary till or dig up the soil.

In the deep mulch method, place the pen over the area where you want to build a garden bed. Just mow the vegetation and leave the clippings in place as a source of nitrogen. The herbaceous layer will decompose rapidly under the mulch with the aid of the bacteria and earthworms that will begin feeding there. This system will build individual raised garden beds wherever you want them.

When Pat and I were building our new house in Charlotte, Vermont, we wanted to start right away to prepare the soil for a salad garden about 10 feet from the back door. We built the house in a meadow containing milkweed, several types of grasses, common vetch and small poplar and green ash saplings. Rather than rent or borrow a rotary tiller to prepare the salad garden spot, we used a chicken tractor.

On the spot where we wanted the salad garden to be, we installed the 40 square foot portable pen and added the waterer and feeder and 20 broilers. The broilers were three weeks old when we started the site, and we kept them there for 5 weeks, adding about an inch of dry hay each day for bedding.

We harvested the chickens on September 1, and moved the pen. The underlying mulch looked like a straw mattress, neatly pressed into shape and about 10-inches deep. When I rolled back the mulch to see underneath, the earthworms, bacteria and fungi had already begun to decompose the mulch. It looked like the inside of a perfectly working compost pile. Next spring this site will be a wonderfully fertile raised bed; ready for growing some of the best salad greens we can hope for.

The top layers of the "mattress" of hay bedding will not decompose into humus by spring. So, we'll layer on about 1-inch of compost or good top soil and plant our salad crops. Within days the sprouted seedlings will send their roots deep into the mulch layer beneath and begin extracting nutrients and moisture.

I've seen this garden method work with hay bales, too. Just set the bales where you want a garden, layer soil on top and plant your crops. The seeds will germinate in the soil layer, then send roots throughout the hay bale in search of nutrients and moisture. Another tip is to use the hay or straw bale as a urinal for a few weeks before planting crops in it. This adds a significant amount of nitrogen that helps break down the carbonaceous straw or hay.

Some folks may have a certain queasiness about using human waste for fertilizer. I think urine from a healthy human is a darn sight better garden fertilizer than some of the chemical stuff you can buy, and it's a lot cheaper. Some of my garden students use urine, diluted with ten parts water, to give their vegetable plots extra nutrients. Just sprinkle the diluted urine on the ground around the plants.

Predators and the Deep Mulch System.

In the deep mulch method, the chickens stay in one spot for several days or even weeks. This invites predators to try to dig under the pen to attack the chickens. Stop burrowing animals by laying chicken wire around the four sides of the pen and anchoring it with clothespins made from old coat hangers. Tuck the wire under the edge of the pen a few inches. Any animal that tries to burrow under the pen will get frustrated by the wire and give up. For more information on predators see Chapter 9.

In extreme cases, particularly with neighborhood dogs, it may be necessary to install a wire or electric fence around the garden perimeter to keep them away from the pen.

Deep Mulch Bedding

Put the 3 week old birds in the pen, along with their furniture (waterer, feeder and roosts). Each day as you tend them just add a new layer of dried hay for bedding. The manure will mix with the hay to form a very well balanced shallow compost pile. It will reach about 8 to 12 inches high during the 5 or 6 weeks you leave the birds in the pen.

The surface of the bedding will remain relatively dry throughout the cycle as long as you keep the lid closed. The tarpaulin on the windward side and on the roof lid will keep most of the rain out. If the bedding does get wet simply add a fresh layer of hay mulch to give the chickens dry footing.

Some moisture will wick up from the ground underneath the mat of bedding. It will not make its way into the top mulch layer, however, because the bedding is not packed tightly enough for capillary action to occur.

Flies and odors can become a problem in the deep mulch system. There are always plenty of flies in the area and the chicken pen attracts them. I think the birds catch all the flies that hatch in the mulch. Adding extra bedding--sometimes even twice a day--will keep the flies from becoming a huge problem. The same thing applies to odors. Just keep adding a little more bedding until you get the right formula. Add extra bedding as the birds get older, especially if the weather is hot. The older chickens excrete more manure, and the bedding can get uncomfortably warm. Just be liberal with the bedding and add it more frequently if you have to.

In the Champlain Valley of Vermont, the spring, summer and fall storms almost invariably come from the South, so we close in the south side of the pen. If a storm does come from another direction we can either put on a temporary tarp to protect the chickens and bedding from getting wet, or we can wait till the rain ends and add fresh, dry bedding.

For a 5 week period with 20 broilers in a 4-by 10-foot chicken tractor we use about 3 bales of mulch hay that we get from a local farmer for $1 per bale. We pull off the blocks (leafs) of hay from the bales and shake them out on the mulch, about 1-inch deep. It works best if you shake bedding on half the pen at a time so the chickens can retreat to the other end of the pen. Once you've placed bedding on the first half of the pen, go to the other end and start shaking bedding there.

An interesting phenomenon is that after a few days the chickens will get very complacent about the new bedding. Often times you'll have to push them out of the way so you can shake the hay or straw over the entire floor. However, if you unexpectedly add something new to the pen it will frighten them and they'll try to run or fly away from it.

I observed this for the first time when Patricia put a stick of firewood in one end of the pen to see if the chickens would roost on it. You would have thought she'd thrown a stick of dynamite in there! The chickens scared away and tried to fly out of the pen. As soon as we took the stick of firewood out, however, they calmed right down and went back to feeding.

If the hay or straw bedding has any seeds in it the chickens will pick them out. They also like to scratch and fluff the bedding so they can lie down in it. Even the cockerels will do this. Unfortunately, there usually isn't enough weed or grain seeds in the hay bedding to add significant feed value.

I think there are lots of opportunities, though, on most small-scale farms to provide supplemental feed for the chickens. It would be an interesting experiment, for example, to grow grain such as millet for the chickens as a "snack." Let the grain mature on the stalk and use the stalk and grain as bedding to see if the chickens will get any feed value from it. Chances are they will peck and scratch through the straw searching out the seeds. This will supplement their diet, and give them some exercise and something to do with their time. The scratching will also help mix the bedding with the manure for better composting.

In his new book *The Contrary Farmer*, author and farmer Gene Logsdon talks about doing this with wheat. His method is to simply cut and bale the wheat—grain and all. Then he feeds it to his hens through the winter. I have fed my hens millet grain mixed in with their feed and notice that they will always peck out the millet seeds first before eating their regular feed.

We always add a smidgen of grit to the feeder lip each day when we add more feed. This is necessary to keep the chicken's digestive system in good working order. In the deep mulch system they don't have much access to dirt or sand to put in their digestive tract. They need this grit to grind their food for digestion. Grit is ground oyster shells and only costs pennies for the amount we give them. It prevents the birds getting impacted craws from too much commercial feed and hay. In larger production facilities, growers offer grit in separate feed trays giving the chickens free access to it.

One way to increase the feed conversion capability of chickens is to harvest green grasses and weeds and put them on top of the fresh bedding. It's a little extra work to do this but the chickens seem to really enjoy pecking at the fresh green grasses. The chlorophyll contained in the green matter is a detoxicant. It helps the chickens' digestive systems expel toxins they might pick up from the feed, from the bedding or from the ground.

Deep Mulch Tractor Size

We put 20 broilers in a 4-by 10-foot pen. This gives them 2 square feet of space each. During their final week of growth the birds may appear a bit crowded, but we've never had any incidents of pecking or fighting. Other pastured poultry growers have been able to reduce pen space to just 1-1/4 square foot per bird without seeing symptoms of over-crowding.

I'm now exploring the idea of starting 30 chickens in this size pen. As they get up to fryer size—2 to 3 pounds dressed weight—I'll harvest 10 of them. I'll leave the remaining 20 chickens in the pen until they reach roasting size of 4-plus pounds dressed weight.

Another way to get fryers and roasters from the same batch of chickens is to buy "straight run" chicks. Straight run means male and female chicks together. About half of them will be male, the other half female. The females grow slower and mature at lower weights than the cockerels. Usually the weight difference is from 1 to 2 pounds.

During the seventh and eighth weeks the cockerels will start learning to crow, so make sure the pens aren't too close to neighbors who complain about the noise. By this time, too, the cockerels are trying to mate the hens. So either harvest the hens for fryers or move them to a different pen and grow them out as egg layers.

The reason I grow some smaller chickens is that I like fried chicken, and I really like to cook chicken on the grill. Unfortunately, the larger pieces from the roaster-sized chickens get over-done on the outside and under-done on the inside when cooked in a frying pan or on the grill.

Deep Mulch System & Your Garden Soil

In this deep mulch method there will be a nitrogen build up in the mulch. At first you might think the extra nitrogen is a great deal higher than your vegetables will need. People have warned me that tomatoes planted in this nitrogen rich bedding will produce all foliage and no fruits.

In my experience this just isn't the case. The high carbon content of the dry hay acts as a superb buffer against a nitrogen overload. As the material breaks down into humus it effectively traps the excess nitrogen and holds it for future crops. The overall effect is that plants extract the nutrients they need without producing excessive foliage. Left over nutrients are held in reserve in the organic matter.

Figure 4: Deep Mulch System

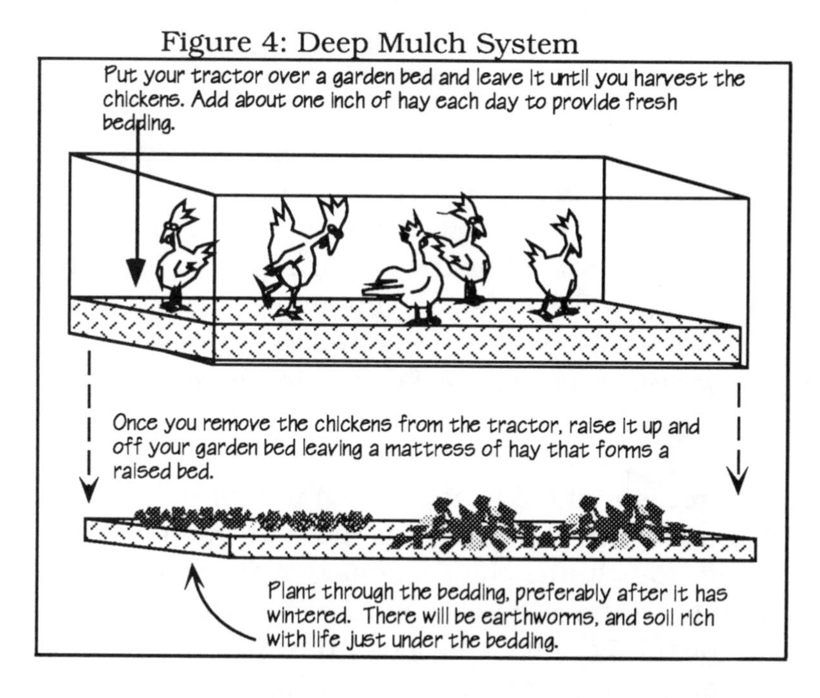

This is not too much nitrogen for crops according to tests at University of Connecticut. After 12 years of compost applications researchers found as much as 2,000 pounds of nitrogen per acre locked in the organic matter in the soil. The bulk of this nitrogen goes to microbes that are busy breaking down the carbon material and releasing the nutrients for crops. In repeated tests, University researchers did not find any instance of excess nitrogen leaching into the ground water. But, their check plots did show leaching activity! They applied 130 pounds per acre of soluble chemical nitrogen fertilizer to the check plots.

To get quick decomposition of the deep mulch it's best to remove the chicken tractor immediately after harvesting the chickens. Water the bed thoroughly. As with a compost pile, the mulch material needs to be moist to start the composting process. A shallow pile will not heat up to the degree a full-sized compost pile will. However it will get warm enough to provide a comfortable environment for the bacteria to do their work of slowly decomposing the material.

Move the chicken tractor off the deep mulch bed as soon as you harvest the chickens. This is to eliminate bacterial attack on frame lumber. This also allows ultraviolet rays and natural rainfall and earth elements to aid in the decomposing process. Also, you might want to use the structure for other purposes such as storage, or cold frame. You might even need the chicken tractor for starting the next batch of chickens.

I haven't measured the heat given off in this slow composting process. I suspect, though, that there is enough heat being generated to help the chickens make it through some of the cool nights we have here in northern Vermont. In warmer regions of the country this potential heating might cause your birds to overheat during extreme hot weather. If this occurs you can buffer the heat by adding more bedding over the manure to act as an insulation blanket.

A way to enhance the structure and fertility of your new garden bed is to layer in some garden soil along with the fresh bedding each day. This garden soil is rich with bacteria and will "seed" the deep mulch. Adding water causes the bacteria to come to life and reduce the pile to finished humus in no time.

Earthworms play a very important role in this decomposition as well. Within only 2 or 3 weeks, even before you remove the chickens, the earthworms will come up in the soil beneath the pen and begin consuming the mulch, turning it into wonderfully rich castings. They will be most active where the deep mulch rests on the soil.

It's best if you can build these deep mulch beds the year before you plant vegetables in them so that the mulch can decay and become nutrient rich humus. However, you can plant in one of these beds before it decomposes if you want. Just shovel in a layer of garden soil or potting mix and set your transplants directly into the new soil.

The layer of grass and weeds that is under the bedding provides the first nitrogen boost to begin sheet composting the bedding. The root system of the native plants will decompose in the soil. This decomposition provides food for the soil dwellers. Channels form as the microbes and earthworms eat the roots. The soil dwellers use these channels for access to the raw materials at the surface. These channels also allow moisture to go up and down, serving as a reservoir to hold water from heavy rainfall.

Putting in layers of bedding each day to balance the nitrogen in the manure will give the optimal carbon to nitrogen ratio of 30:1, for great compost. At this rate you are adding the equivalent of 40 cubic yards of compost per acre, enough to assure you of optimal yields from your vegetable garden.

Deep Mulch System Daily Care

Daily care for the 20 broilers in the deep mulch pen requires nothing more than visiting them once each day and adding more feed in the feeder, giving them fresh water, and putting down fresh bedding. It takes only a minute to wash and fill the waterer if you have a garden hose close by. Keeping the feed in a sealed container next to the chicken tractor makes refilling the chicken feeder quick and simple. Store the hay or straw on a pallet near by so you can replenish the chicken bedding quickly. You can do all these daily chores in less than 5 minutes. If you also throw in some harvested greens it might add another minute to your schedule. These are ideal tasks for youngsters to help you with.

We store our mulch hay bales on a pallet next to the chicken tractor so that it is easy and convenient to add bedding to the pen as needed. We cover the stored bales with a small tarp and tie the corners to the underlying pallet so the tarp doesn't blow off in a strong wind.

Figure 5: Feed and Hay Storage for Easy Daily Care

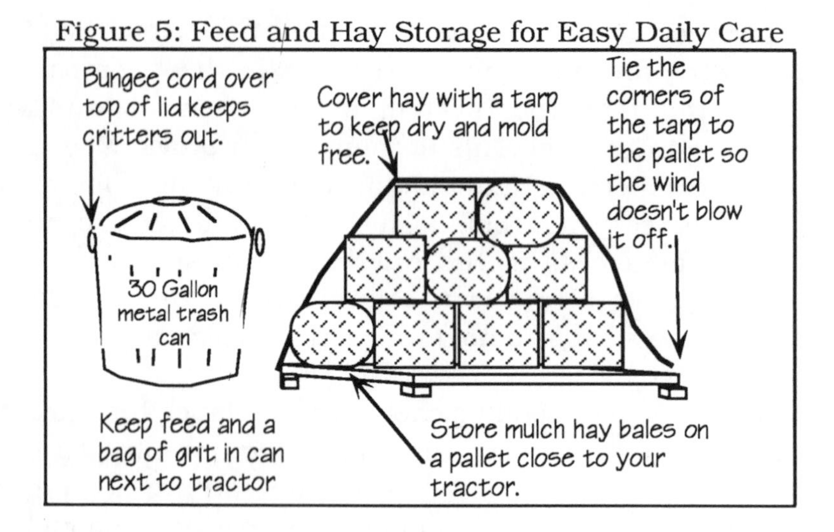

We keep our feed in a galvanized trash can next to the deep mulch pen. We keep the lid on with a strong bungee cord to keep raccoons out. It's a simple matter to scoop out fresh feed each day.

We also keep a small bag of crushed clam shells or gravel in the feed barrel and mix it in with the feed so the chickens will have access to grit. This helps their digestive system since they don't have access to natural grit.

Add a Cold-Frame to Create a Portable Bio-Shelter.
One way to get maximum usage of your chicken tractor is to reverse its orientation during the spring and fall. By putting the enclosed side on the North you will protect the chickens from cold northerly breezes. With the open side on the South they will get warm sunlight throughout most of the day. When the sun gets too hot for them in mid-summer, just rotate the pen and put the enclosed side to the South so the chickens are in the shade.

In the spring and fall you can also put a solar cold frame on the south side of the chicken tractor. The tractor box will serve as a reflector and sun trap for the sun's heat, and will protect the cold frame from the north wind. There is a potential here, too, for the birds to help heat the cold frame and provide some carbon dioxide for the growing plants.

Figure 6: Tractor with Solar Cold Frame

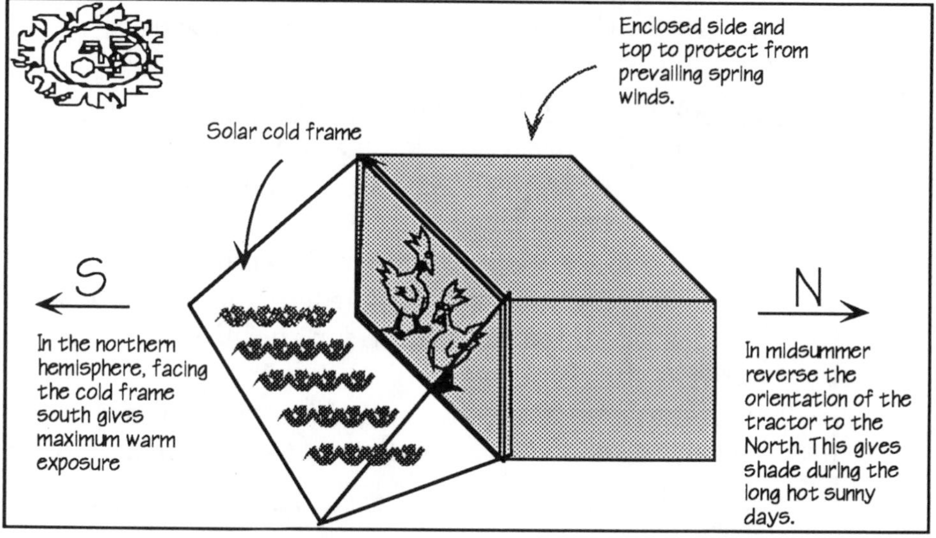

Remove the tarp on the south side of the chicken tractor and snuggle the pen against the north side of the cold frame. The chicken wire on the side of the pen remains in place to keep the chickens from having access to the plants in the cold frame. The plastic film on the cold frame will protect the chickens from the chilly wind.

You can make the cold frame, and the chickens, warmer by putting a tarp on the north side of the shelter-pen, and at the ends. This will block the cold air from hitting the chickens and the plants. The table below lists the reciprocal benefits and advantages of this "bio-shelter".

The cold frame can measure 40 square feet, the same size as the chicken tractor. The cold frame will produce about $50 worth of lettuce during the time the birds are growing to harvestable size. Sell the lettuce to the folks who buy the chickens from you. It is also possible to start seedlings such as broccoli or, better yet, tomatoes, in the cold frame part of the portable bio-shelter. After harvesting the chickens, remove the cold frame and turn the site into a permanent garden bed with plants already planted and growing.

Table 5: Advantages of a Bio-Shelter

1. Heat and light for the chickens and the plants.
2. Carbon dioxide from the chickens exchanges for oxygen from the plants.
3. Plants and chickens have northerly wind break.
4. The close proximity of the garden and the chickens provides an activities center for the grower to do all chores at the same location.
5. This synergistic association makes wonderful use of the chicken tractor system. This becomes a portable or at least semi-portable, bio-shelter.

Another example of stacking in time and place, is to add a trellis to the south side of the chicken tractor for growing vining crops such as green beans, cucumbers or indeterminate tomatoes. This will provide shade for the chickens during the hotter days of summer.

Don't attach the vining crop to the chicken tractor frame, though. It will harbor moisture that can lead to decaying wood frame members. Also, some vining crops, particularly peas, are hard to remove from trellis netting when they die. It's easier if you can simply take the trellis down and clean the dead vines into your compost pile.

3. Sheet Mulch System - Halfway Between Grazing and Deep Mulch

In the sheet mulch system we think of using the chicken tractor more than one day but less than a month on each position. The objectives are:

1. Kill the grass and weeds in the garden bed.
2. Fertilize the garden bed.
3. Build up a layer of organic matter (mulch) that will hold the nutrients and protect the soil from erosion and drying out.
4. Add fertility and organic matter to the soil as the mulch decays and turns into humus.

Begin by putting the chickens on the garden bed where they will deposit a layer of manure. Add mulch to the manure each day until the mulch measures about 4-inches deep, about as high as the base board on the pen. Then, move the chickens to the next spot and repeat the process.

This sequence adds loads of organic matter and manure to several different beds while the broilers are in the garden. If you are using laying hens in the portable pen you can cover far more ground each year, since the hens can be in the chicken tractor for up to nine months. In most areas of the country you can keep chickens outside from six to nine months.

The chickens drop manure where you need it, and the mulch holds the nitrogen and other nutrients in a stable condition while the mulch slowly decays. This lets the gardener forego planting cover crops altogether, and still gives the grower the opportunity to move the pens regularly to benefit from the manure applications.

The traditional way of converting a sod lawn area to garden beds is to rotary till the site repeatedly, killing the grass and mixing it with the soil. Rotary tilling is noisy, time consuming, energy intensive and expensive and destroys the soil structure and tilth. There's a better way to create garden beds, using chicken tractors. Put the chickens on the site for about 2 to 3 days. They will eat all the grass right down to bare ground and leave a thick layer of manure. Then move the tractor to the next site, and mulch the one they were just on. When the next batch of chickens arrives 30 days later, just put them on the existing mulch.

This way, a continuous rich mulch is being placed on each garden bed. This mulch kills the sod underneath and allows the soil life to do its job of decomposing the leaves and root mass, turning them into fertile humus.

No tillage at all is required. Just plant the crops through the mulch. Use the chickens this way to rid the beds of weeds and grasses during the first batch. The following batches just add more fertility and mulch to each bed, making them super rich and super productive for the following year's vegetable crop.

In this model the grower will have to feed more grain since there is less graze for the birds. The saved labor of tilling and planting cover crops after each rotation of birds will offset the extra feed bill. At best we can only hope to save 36-cents per bird if they are eating grass and weeds. We can save at least that much if we don't have to rotary till and buy cover crop seed. In addition, the following year when the field is ready to plant to vegetables, there will be no need to mow and till under a heavy cover crop. To start seedlings, just pull back the mulch and set the transplants, then push the mulch back around them.

A word here about cover crops. For many years I believed, like most of my peers, that cover crops were an effective way to add organic matter to the soil. Recently, however, I've talked with researchers at the University of Vermont who believe that, in many cases, organic matter in the soil does not increase significantly by tilling under cover crops.

What seems to happen instead, is that the act of tilling introduces air to the soil. This then causes an explosion of microbiotic life that quickly consumes the newly introduced organic matter. This is particularly true with succulents such as buckwheat which add very little if any organic matter to the soil since they are mostly water. Additionally, the extra tillage required to kill and cover the green manure crop causes loss of soil structure and tilth. Over the years I've observed that our favorite cover crop, winter rye, is very hard to kill and will sometimes resprout in the vegetable beds. The repeated tilling necessary to kill the rye damages the soil more than the value of the rye as a green manure. This isn't to say, though, that cover crops are useless. Far from it. They just aren't the panacea for poor soil we once thought they were.

One researcher told me that he now favors simply mowing the cover crop and leaving the biomass on the surface where it breaks down slowly. When you study natural systems this is what you see. Annuals die in the fall and form a mulch on the soil, which protects it from the elements. As time goes by the soil microbes and earthworms and other mulch-dwellers slowly turn the mulch into humus. This leads me to believe that top soil doesn't deepen, it uppens.

Mulch, whether left from dead cover crops such as oats—or straw and leaves spread by the gardener—will keep the ground cooler in the early spring. This can be an advantage in warmer climates in the summer time, but a disadvantage in cooler climates in the spring.

Having mulch on your garden beds may mean you will have to delay planting some of your crops until the soil has warmed. That's not too big a problem, though. My experience has been that the later planted crops almost invariably mature on or near the same day as crops planted earlier in unmulched soil. I think this may have to do with the mulch preventing the ground from freezing to deeper levels than unmulched soil, and thus thawing earlier in the spring.

Some beds will require a fine seed bed for small seeds such as carrots, beets, scallions, radishes and so forth. Just spread a light layer of compost, about 1/2 inch deep, over the sheet mulch. Broadcast the seeds, then cover them with another light layer of compost. Seeds sprout and send out roots that penetrate the sheet mulch to the soil underneath and find a wealth of nutrients there for quick and healthy growth. The result, no tillage at all. Great!

Crops you can transplant through the mulch are potatoes, pumpkins, winter squash, summer squash, tomatoes, eggplants, peppers, cucumbers, lettuce, broccoli, kale, collards and so on.

Leave the paths between the garden beds in grass and white clover. Mow these periodically and leave the clippings on the ground to fertilize the grass. You can also use the grass clippings to spike your compost pile, or feed the clippings to the chickens.

Each sheet-mulch-chicken-tractor with 20 chickens in it will need about 3 bales of mulch hay to carry it through the rotation. Mulch hay, costing $1 per bale, adds $3 to the cost of the batch. With chickens dressing out at 4 pounds each, that's 80 pounds of meat, with the mulch hay adding about 4-cents per pound to the overall cost of the dressed weight of the birds.

In a sheet mulch system, each batch moves 5 times, so each 40 square foot pen will cover 200 square feet per batch. With three batches per season you will cover 600 square feet per season. A typical home garden today is less than 600 square feet. The garden can get most of the soil fertility and most of the replacement organic matter from the chickens in this system.

This method even works on a one-day only basis. Move the chickens to fresh graze daily and let them reduce the spot to bare ground and cover it with nitrogen rich manure. Move them to their next position. Instead of spreading cover crop seed and tilling, cover the disturbed area with a layer of hay mulch about 1-inch deep. This will act as a buffer to hold the nutrients in the upper levels of the soil and will provide carbonaceous materials for the soil life to use while reducing the mulch to humus. This can provide a very rich soil in no time at all.

As the second and following batches of chickens arrive at this spot in their rotation you will enhance the fertility of the soil tremendously. If you start a second batch of chickens on the site and the hay mulch remaining from the preceding batch is wet, you may want to put down a light layer of new mulch hay to keep the chickens dry.

This does of course nullify any gain from grazing, but conversely you don't have to buy cover crop seed and spend the time needed to spread it and till it under. The mulch will cost some money but chances are the saved labor is worth more to you than the cost of the mulch. Think about the graze the same way. You'll have more feed to buy, but will spend less time tilling under the plots.

There is another way to approach this. Use cover crops on three batches of chickens. Harvest the third batch and put down the mulch. Let it set through the winter until next spring. During the winter the mulch will have time to decompose and will add tremendously to the enrichment of the soil. All of the mulch will not be decomposed come spring. You have the option of either tilling in the remaining mulch for a seed bed, or you can simply plant your transplants right through the mulch that remains. This can work too, if you are converting pasture or lawn to garden. The over-wintering mulch will kill the grass underneath, making it much easier for you to prepare a seed bed in the spring.

Shelter-Pens Larger Than 4-feet wide

Several of my friends are using larger pens, measuring 10-by 10-feet or 10- by 12-feet. These larger pens have either a flat roof or a hooped roof. The advantage, of course, of the larger pens is that they are relatively inexpensive to build. They will hold more chickens, and can cover more ground quickly if you are raising your chickens in a pasture situation.

However, there are some disadvantages to the larger pens, particularly the hoop style portable pens. First, of course, is that they don't fit over your garden beds when you want to preserve permanent pathways between beds. There's also the difficulty of moving them, since they can be quite heavy and bulky, making them awkward to handle.

Also—especially with the hooped roof pen—you have to climb inside them each day to fill the waterer and the feeder. When you want to catch the birds you have to crawl around inside. Of course, you can always build a flat-roofed pen. Put a panel in the top of the unit so you reach through from the top.

I've found that the hoop style pens are more expensive and much harder to build than the flat roofed pens. Possibly the only advantage I can think of for the hoop style pens is that you can also use them as portable greenhouses and field tunnels by removing the tarpaulin and replacing it with plastic greenhouse film. You can easily do this with flat roofed pens, too. They will shed water almost as easily as a hoop roofed pen.

Another style of pen, like my folks used to use, is the A-frame on skids. This style is easy to build, but hard to manage. I don't use it because the steep roof eliminates a lot of head room inside, and it's very difficult to get at the waterer and feeder, or to catch the chickens at harvest time.

I haven't converted my poultry operation to larger shelter-pens because I use the tractors on 4-foot wide beds. It isn't any great bother to move the chicken tractor across the pathway to begin the next pass on the adjacent garden bed. The goal in using the tractors on the garden beds is to get the paths and beds into a permanent state so that the soil does not have to be rotary tilled. The soil just gets healthier and healthier each year.

This makes for a much more attractive and abundant garden. The mulched permanent garden beds look very nice next to the grassy permanent paths. The grassy paths also give us an excellent avenue to walk to our birds and garden beds without getting muddy feet or encouraging erosion from either water or wind.

4. Intensive Grazing in Paddocks

The English Pop Hole method is worth discussing here simply because it is the forerunner of the chicken tractor. The Pop Hole method relies on short duration intensive grazing in rotated paddocks. English poultry growers use this method to raise thousands of birds per year with good results. By law English growers can carry only 400 hens per acre in this method, or double that for broilers. The obvious reason for the limit on birds has to do with the toxicity of the soil after growing so many birds on such a small piece of land.

The way this system works is to place the portable shelter in the center of the area for grazing, then erect portable electric fencing in a square area around the shelter. There are four pop holes, one at each corner of the shelter. Close all but one door, thereby directing the birds to graze in the specified area. Depending on your creativity, this scheme can be more elaborate, with as many individual paddocks and doors as you can fit into your site.

Once the chickens finish grazing the first group of paddocks, move the whole shelter and pen system to the next location and repeat the process, on and on across the field. At some point, after the grass has recovered from grazing, you will be able to return your flock to the beginning point and start the rotation all over.

Figure 7: Hen House with Rotational Paddocks

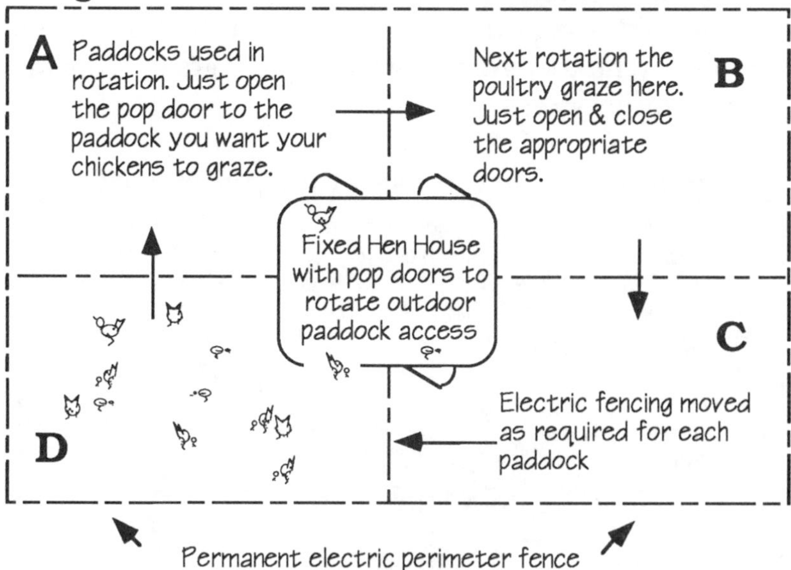

Another design option for the pop hole method is to have a long, enclosed wire tunnel running out from the hen house and perpendicular to the garden beds. At each garden bed there is a pop hole in the tunnel. A second tunnel rests perpendicular to the main tunnel. It moves from bed to bed as needed. The chickens enter the garden bed tunnel through the pop hole. Some folks call this the permaculture method. Its only difference from the English Pop Hole method is the addition of the long service tunnel at the head of the garden beds.

I've never used the Enlish pop hole method for raising poultry, so I don't feel competent to recommend it. Common sense tells me there are several disadvantages that most probably outweigh the advantages of scale and low cost.

To begin with, when you turn hens or broilers out to graze, their natural tendency is to stay close to the shelter. They graze areas close to the shelter down to bare dirt. The undergrazed growth just a few feet away will grow large and become so rank the birds won't want to eat it. Then you have to mow or scythe the clumps of weeds and grass. This makes more work for less return.

Figure 8: Fixed Hen House with Moveable Tunnels

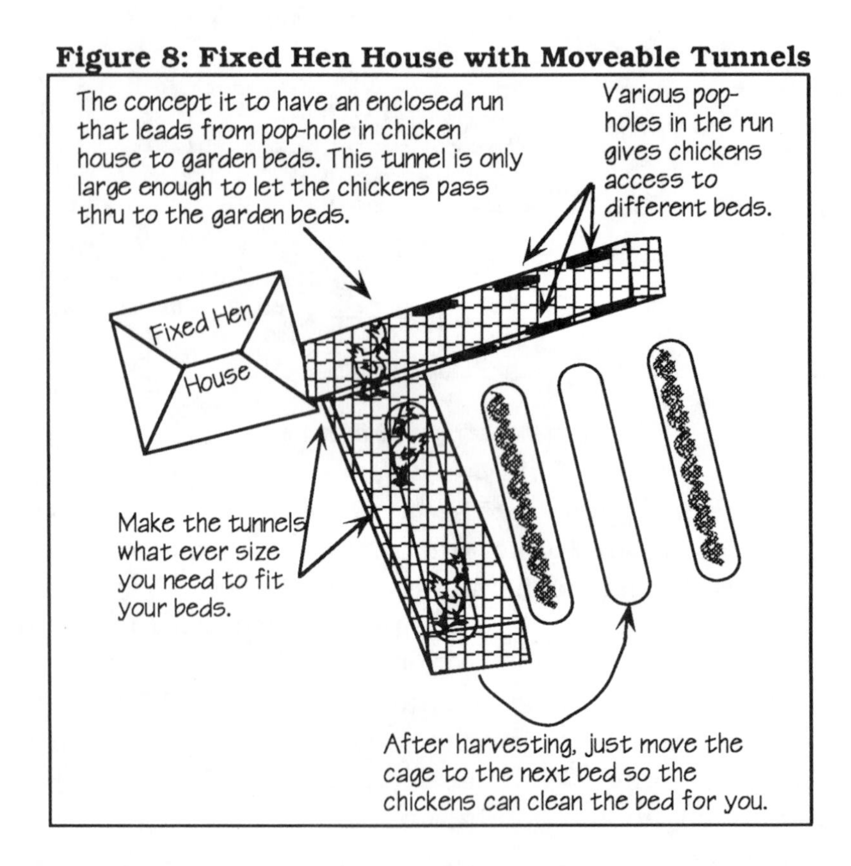

This consideration becomes doubly important if you are raising hybrid breeds that have had their natural foraging characteristics bred out of them. I've seen many times, and had other growers tell me, that most of the hybrids will refuse to graze altogether. Unless you force them to graze by withholding feed temporarily and setting the birds directly on the grass you want them to eat. I have raised hybrid Cornish Cross broilers that were so lethargic they refused to eat potato beetles or earthworms that I collected and placed in their pen.

A second disadvantage is the open pens used in the English pop hole system don't protect the chickens from flying predators such as hawks and owls, or from wild birds that might be diseased.

Another concern is that the birds will graze their favorite plants exclusively, allowing the undesired plants to overtake and crowd out the desired plants over one or two grazing seasons. It is necessary to keep the paddock size small and the number of birds high to force them to graze all the plants in the paddock. By doing this you will certainly encourage diversity in the grasses and herbaceous forbs, and year after year the graze will get better.

One of my favorite farm writers, Gail Damerow, has used this method for her portable pullet house. She finds that the area where the coop was takes a long time to regrow, sometimes more than a year, due to compaction and excessive nitrogen.

Finally, the sheer cost of building the hen house and associated chicken runs can be prohibitive. I talked with one grower who has spent over $800 and a week of labor to build an 8- by 12-foot hen house and 25- by 50-foot run. This set-up will only house 50 laying hens. For that amount of money I think he could have built a dozen chicken tractors that would be far more portable and useful in the garden.

The size of a hen house is dictated by the size of the farmer who has to get inside to tend the chickens and gather eggs. Hens don't need an 8-foot ceiling. It's much less expensive to build a chicken-size house than a people-size house. With the chicken tractors just lift the lid and reach in.

5. Polyface Model - Poultry with Beef Cattle.
Joel and Teresa Salatin at Polyface Farm in Sloop, Virginia, have developed an entire livelihood on just 20 acres, using a unique combination of free range beef cattle and chicken tractors. Polyface Farm (*farm of many faces*) specializes in raising the "best poultry, rabbits, lamb and beef in the world" according to their recently published book, *Pastured Poultry Profit$*. The subtitle of their book is *Net $25,000 in 6 months on 20 acres.*

They are in the Shenandoah Valley of Virginia at 2000' elevation, and grow as many as 10,000 broilers per year using portable, flat-roofed pens measuring 10-feet by 12-feet.

They refer to their method as pastured poultry. The Salatins range their chickens in conjunction with their high density, short duration beef grazing. They prepare the grass by grazing the beef cattle ahead of the chickens. The advantage is that chickens graze best when the grass is fairly short, about up to their bellies.

As the chickens follow behind the beef, they peck and scratch through the cow manure, scattering it over a larger area and digging out any worm or fly larvae in the manure. This breaks the cycle of bovine stomach parasites, eliminating the need for synthetic worm medicines for the cows.

The chickens scatter the manure piles, eliminating the concentration of nitrogen in one spot that will cause heavily nitrogenated grass to regrow. The cows refuse to eat these overly-lush clumps of grass. Joel calls these areas the "repugnance zone".

According to Joel, there is another advantage of chickens grazing after the beef cattle. The enzymes in cow manure are perfectly balanced for the chickens' digestive system. The enzymes help the chickens digest their food. In nature the birds always follow the ruminants. Wild birds always follow deer and elk, for example. The Cattle Egret got its name from its habit of foraging with cattle.

To encourage the chickens to eat more grass, the Salatins withhold grain feed for the first 1/2 hour each morning after they move the chicken pens. They also move the older broilers twice daily to spread their manure better and to encourage even more grazing. These frequent moves keep the birds cleaner, especially in rainy weather. Moving the heavy birds more frequently also helps keep them from killing the pasture grasses and forbs. Joel feels the primary benefits of this system are that there is no manure to haul out, or flies to control, and all the nutrient laden manure is going directly to growing vegetation.

Using this method, the Salatins work hard for six months during the growing season, then take the rest of the year off. They still manage to earn more than $25,000 per year from their 20 acre farm. They process the chickens at the farm, and sell them to a group of loyal clientele who drive to the farm several times each season to pick up their dressed broilers and eggs. They started their whole farm poultry operation for about what it would cost to buy a used, mid-size farm tractor.

While Joel relies on Cornish Cross hybrids for fryers and broilers, he turns to the classic American poultry breeds for egg layers. He feels their aggressive foraging characteristics combined with their hardiness and weathering abilities make them far more suitable for free range egg farming than any of the modern hybrid egg layers. His favorites are Dominique, New Hampshire and Rhode Island Reds. Joel claims these birds will range out 200 yards from their shelter and will consume significant quantities of protein laden worms, crickets, grasshoppers and larvae, as much as 7 pounds per 100 chickens per day.

Joel doesn't use any electric fencing around his laying hens. Instead, he relies on their natural homing instinct to go back to their egg mobile shelter at night, where he closes them in before the night predators come calling. He doesn't worry about hawks and owls because the chickens are large enough and aggressive enough to fend for themselves during the day time.

6. Hens on Wheels.

Egg producer's can use the chicken tractor on wheels to move their hens to any place in the garden or yard that seems appropriate. Ed Robinson, author of the classic homesteader's manual, *The Have More Plan*, has developed plans for an ingenious mobile chicken coop. There is a complete set of plans for Robinson's hen house on wheels in Will Graves' book, *Raising Poultry Successfully.* (see appendix).

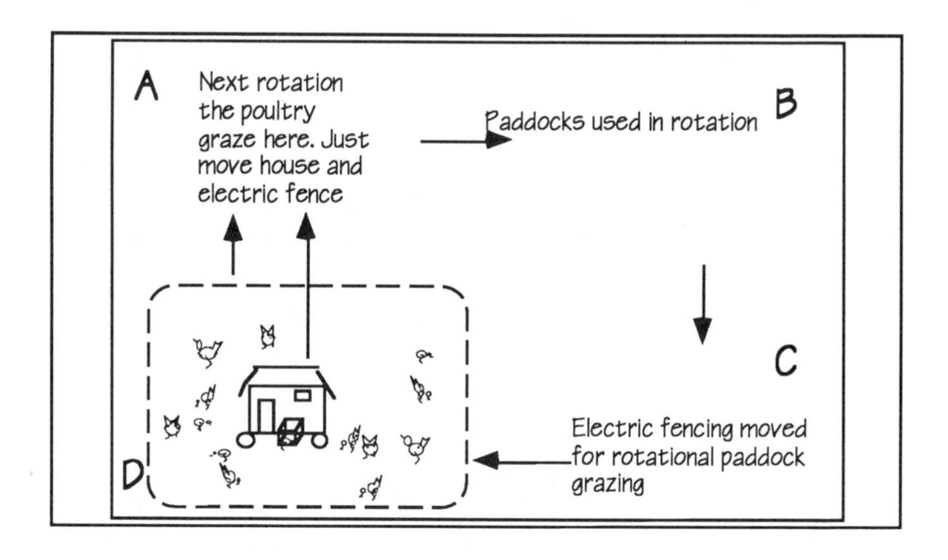

7. The Greenhouse System

Can you raise chickens in your greenhouse? Yes! It's a natural combination. You get oxygen from plants and carbon dioxide from the chickens. Plants need carbon dioxide and chickens need oxygen. The manure adds nitrogen and other valuable nutrients to the greenhouse soil. Use the bedding to biofilter the ammonia and other gasses given off by the manure.

The chickens also give body heat to help keep the greenhouse warm. Using this model you can keep your laying hens out in the garden beds through spring, summer and fall, and in the greenhouse through the winter. This provides an excellent use of fall and early-spring greenhouse space. Then use the greenhouse in the summer for producing field tunnel crops.

My first experience with raising chickens in the greenhouse came about with Tim Laird, former manager of Intervale Community Farm in Burlington, Vermont. He turned seven of his chickens into a 12-foot by 30-foot greenhouse, thinking they would glean the weeds and grasses during the fall and early winter.

In a 360 square foot greenhouse, seven hens were just not enough to get the job done. They hung around the water bucket and feed trough, only eating the tender grasses and weeds within easy reach. The weeds at the back of the greenhouse grew large and rank and the chickens simply ignored them.

From this experience we learned that to get clean weed and grass control from chickens it is necessary to confine them for short periods of time on fairly small sections of the greenhouse floor. This forces them, in a sense, to eat all the green vegetation that is there, and causes the manure to be spread more equitably throughout the greenhouse.

Now I use the "under-the-bench plan" for raising poultry in a 12- by 12-foot greenhouse. Starting about mid-March, I start early seedlings in the greenhouse and fence in the space under the benches. It is a great place to grow chicks using the deep mulch system. By the time the seedlings are ready to go to the garden the chickens are old enough to move outside to chicken tractors.

During the summer I remove the benches from the greenhouse and use the deep mulch beds to raise greenhouse tomatoes, cucumbers or herbs and salad greens. By early winter, when the greenhouse requires heat, I move the chickens back inside and let them stay in there for the winter. Then, the following spring I move the greenhouse to a new location, turn its former site into garden beds, and start the whole rotation all over.

This method will also work very well with hydroponic or soil-less mix crops that grow on the benches while the chickens remain beneath the benches. With this type system you can have virtually year round egg, vegetable and salad green production.

In some circumstances, for instance if you are using the greenhouse for winter shelter for your hens, you can fasten portable outside runs to the greenhouse to enable chickens to have access to outside graze. These runs will become heavily enriched areas that can become future raised beds.

It's important to install motorized vent fans in the greenhouse to keep the chickens from overheating on warm, sunny days. Their own body heat will often be enough to warm the greenhouse during all but the coldest days of winter, particularly if they are one of the old standard breed chickens that are hardy.

According to Anna Eddy, owner of the Solviva Greenhouse on Martha's Vineyard, Massachusetts, heat gain from chickens will amount to 8 btu's per pound of animal per hour. Each chicken provides heat in the equivalent of 2.5 gallons of heating oil per heating season. This enables chickens to survive temperatures down to 0 degrees F without undue stress.

Use electric varmint fencing around the permiter to stop predators that might claw through the plastic film. One grower I know, Matt and Scout Proft in Dorset, Vermont, built their greenhouse up on a foundation so the coyotes couldn't dig in to get at the baby turkeys.

The greenhouse is an excellent example of "stacking space" by having chickens on the floor and seedlings on the benches. It's also an example of "time stacking" since we are growing baby chickens while seedlings are growing as the succession crop for the greenhouse. You can even use this greenhouse space to grow the baby chicks you will be moving to your broiler pens later in the season.

Economics of a Market Garden Bio-Shelter

Let's take a look at what sort of income you can anticipate from a simple hoop style greenhouse measuring 12-feet by 12-feet. This gives you 144 square feet of sheltered space, but you'll need some of it for pathways and door access.

This size greenhouse can have 4-foot wide benches running down each side of a 4-foot pathway. Under these benches you will have room to grow 48 broilers or 24 laying hens.

For this exercise let's assume you will grow one batch of broilers in the spring while your seedlings are growing on the benches. Once the seedlings go to the garden you can move the broilers to an outside shelter-pen or process them for the freezer. Then move the benches out of the greenhouse. Double dig the area under the benches and shape it into growing beds. These growing beds, enriched by the chicken manure and bedding, make an excellent place to grow tomatoes in the greenhouse. Sometimes there is too much mulch to be turned under for garden beds. You can remove the excess mulch and use it in your garden or put it on the compost pile.

With 96 square feet of bed space you can grow 24 tomato plants that will yield about 20 pounds per plant. This will give you a total harvest of 480 pounds. These tomatoes will sell for $1.50 per pound average, bringing in $720 in tomato sales.

You can sell your 48 broilers for $8 each for a total broiler income of $384. Additionally, you have 96 square feet of bench space. In this amount of room you can grow a total of

3456 seedlings valued at wholesale at 15 cents each—making them worth $520.

So, your potential gross income from the greenhouse over an eight month period is:

Seedlings	$520
Broilers	$384
Tomatoes	$720
Total	$1,624

This gives you a total income of $11.28 per square foot. Also, you'll have 96 square feet of incredibly rich garden beds for future garden crops.

You didn't have to spend a great amount of money to make over $1,600 from your greenhouse. You didn't need to buy any heavy equipment, or go to any great trouble to accomplish all of this. The greenhouse itself can cost as little as $200 to $300 if you build it yourself. In some areas of the country you can pay the taxes on your house with just one 12 x 12 greenhouse. At the very least you can enjoy a great little spare time income for only an hour or so of work each day. You might spend about 100 hours over the course of the season doing all these things and expect to earn better than $10 per hour from your hobby business, after paying all expenses.

Use the chicken tractor greenhouse as the center piece of your market garden. Expand your garden each year with chickens preparing land as you need it. Sell some of your produce to make this a business venture that will give you a tax write-off that helps overcome the tax bite on your regular, full time income from your real job. It's a great way to practice and develop skills for future farming adventures, as well.

For more information on market gardening for income, refer to my book *Backyard Market Gardening*, (see appendix).

Chapter 3: Here's How to Build Your Custom Chicken Tractor

Before designing the pen, you need to know the needs (what goes in) and products (what comes out) of the chicken tractor system you envision. There are many, many questions you'll want to ask and answer as you design your shelter-pen. Some of them are:

1. How many chickens do you need to feed your family or to sell each year?
2. Do you want to grow egg layers, fryers, broilers or all three?
3. Which breed?
4. Which chicken tractor system?
5. What materials are available and what more will you need?
6. Size of garden and how big do you want it to become?

For this example, let's consider building a chicken tractor like the one I use in my own garden. This exercise will help you determine just what your needs are and what you hope to accomplish with your portable shelter-pen.

Let's assume you want to raise 20 broilers for your own freezer. You might also want to grow enough extra broilers to sell to friends and neighbors. This way you can earn the money to recover your start up costs. In this example, you'll need to grow 40 extra chickens to sell in order to break even financially.

Since each batch of broilers will be in the brooder for 3 weeks and in the tractor for 5 weeks, it's possible to get four or even five batches in rotation during a long season. In Vermont where I live we have a fairly short growing season, so I only plan on growing 3 batches per season in each chicken tractor. If your season is similar, you can plan on growing 3 batches of 20 chickens each, keeping 20 for your own use and selling 40 to pay the costs of the operation.

Further, let's assume you have a garden like mine, that has 4-foot wide growing beds that are 20 feet long. There are grassy pathways between the beds. If you are using a typical 4-foot by 10-foot chicken tractor that covers 40 square feet, and you want to move the chicken tractor each day, you will need a total of 1,400 square feet to graze your chickens. If you move the chickens every other day instead of daily you will only need 700 square feet of garden space.

You arrive at this figure by multiplying the size of the portable pen times the number of batches per season times 35 days of grazing per batch. In other words: 40 square feet x 3 batches x 35 days (divided by 2) = 700 square feet. This does not include the space required for your pathways.

Learn By Doing

It's easy to get carried away with the building of these chicken tractors. The first one I made is very sturdy, but so heavy it takes two or even three of us to move it, with much huffing and puffing and jostling. My first generation pen is 3-1/2 feet high, 4 feet wide and 12-1/2 feet long. The frame is 2-inch by 4-inch boards, with 3/8-inch plywood nailed on the north end and west side, and half of the east side.

On this early prototype the top is framed with 2-by 4-inch boards, with the north half covered with plywood and the south half covered with 1-inch poultry netting. The pen has 1-inch poultry netting on the south end and half of the east side, where the plywood covering ends. The plywood is exterior grade and stained with a wood preserving stain. While this pen is far too heavy for use as a portable chicken tractor, it still works as a deep mulch pen and as a semi-portable brooder pen.

Figure 9: Second Generation Chicken Tractor

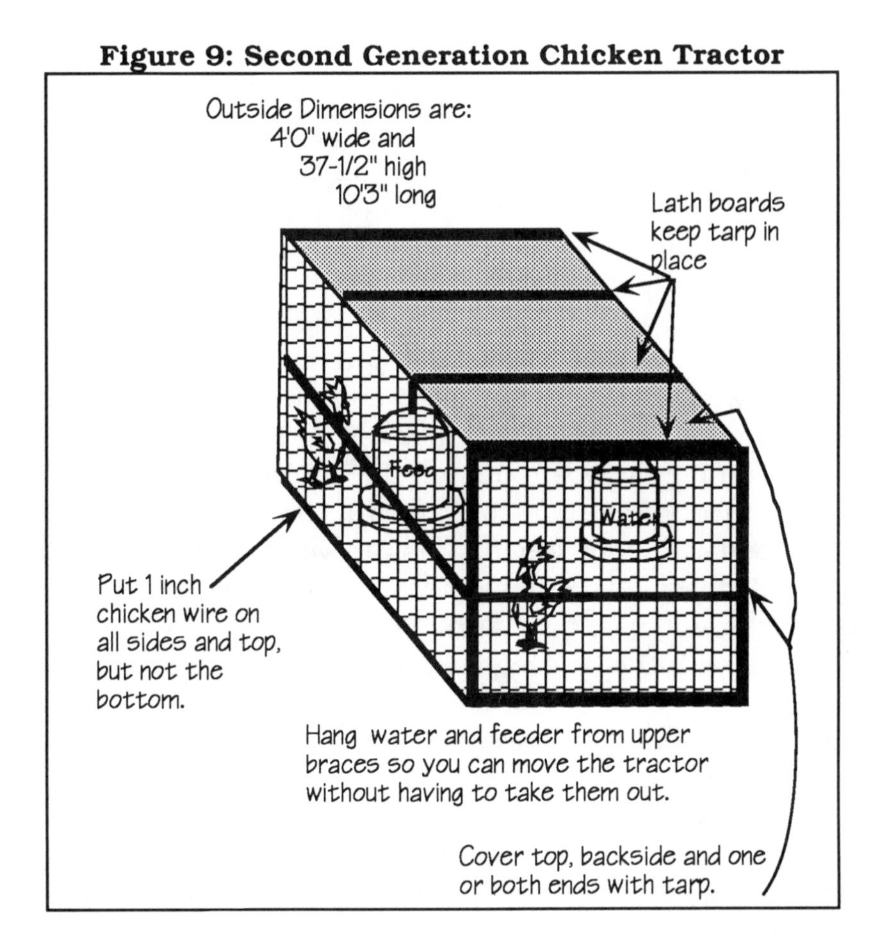

The second-generation portable pen I now use is 3 feet high, 4-feet wide and 10-feet long. I wrap the pen with chicken wire then cover it with poly tarp. I use the 3-feet height because that's the standard height of the 1-inch poultry netting that we use to surround the sides and ends of the pen. Three feet is also a good height for hanging the waterer and feeder from the upper cross brace. There is no bottom wire installed because we want the chickens to have access to the ground beneath the pen.

Use 1-inch galvanized chicken wire for the chicken tractors. The larger 2-inch poultry netting is not suitable since smaller varmints such as weasels can easily get into the cage. With the 2-inch openings the little chicks can get out and raccoons can reach in. Secure the wire carefully to the pen with galvanized poultry staples. Some of the varmints that will try to get into the pen are quite strong, raccoons especially, and can easily rip the staples out unless you hammer them in securely.

Cover the whole pen, except the bottom, with chicken wire, and the windward side and both ends with a polypropylene tarpaulin, held in place with staples and lath boards nailed to the framing members. Install the poultry netting (chicken wire) to the roof lid then cover it with the poly tarp. The tarp is inexpensive, light weight, easy to work with, waterproof, and provides shade and wind protection. I used blue tarp on the first prototypes, but I find I like green tarps better. Green blends in with the landscape better than blue does.

Other coverings you might consider using are tin or fiberglass roofing or thin plywood sealed for weather protection. Joel Salatin uses tin roofing exclusively but I've never tried it. I have tried plywood and found it to be too heavy. I've never used fiberglass panels because I think they are too expensive.

I'm now considering making all my future portable pens with panels bolted together so I can disassemble them in the fall for winter storage out of the weather. This will extend their life a great deal. Even without winter storage out of the elements, these pens will last from 5 to 10 years with only minor maintenance each year.

In the early part of the season you can use the chicken tractor as a sun trap or wind break for growing plants. You can use the pen for firewood storage, too. A 4- x 10-foot pen that is 3' high will hold 1 cord of firewood. If you remove the poly tarp and replace it with plastic greenhouse film you can use this chicken tractor as a cold frame or grow tunnel.

I have built all my pens with flat roofs. I find that water runs off the roof easily. Adding a sloped, peaked or rounded roof to the portable pen is extra work and expense and not at all necessary.

Figure 10: Tractor Winter Storage

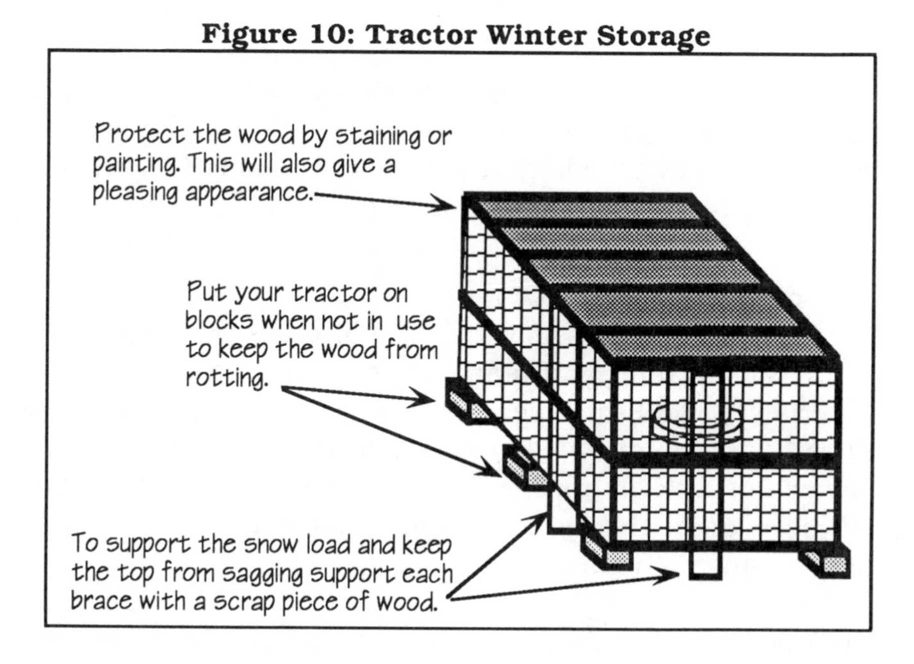

Over the winter set the chicken tractor up on blocks to keep the wooden frame from contacting the ground and getting wet and rotting. The chicken wire and tarpaulin covers will last for many years exposed to the weather as long as they aren't damp for extended periods of time. In the winter support the flat, hinged lid against heavy snow loads. I just prop a scrap board under each cross brace.

1. Size, Configuration, Space per Bird

Each broiler requires 1.5 to 2 square feet of space for optimal growth and ease of management. In a 4-foot by 10-foot tractor you can easily grow 20 birds each flight. Laying hens need twice as much space to be comfortably uncrowded, so plan on having only 10 hens in this size pen. You can start two or three times this many chickens in the pen. As they grow larger you will want to separate some of them into other pens, or sell them.

Turkeys are much larger and need at least four times more room to maneuver in the pen. In this 4-foot by 10-foot pen you will do best with only 2 or 3 turkeys. If you want to grow the large turkey breeds that have a wing span of 6-feet, you might consider using a larger pen, say 10- by 10-feet.

2. Construction materials

You can build your 4-foot by 10-foot chicken tractor on a Saturday morning and start using it that very afternoon. Materials to build the pen will cost less than $75 in most parts of the country. Plan to stain or paint your chicken tractor for uniform appearance and weather protection. You will need to let the paint or stain dry for at least 24 hours before using the pen.

The keys to building a successful portable pen are to make it light enough to be portable, heavy enough to withstand repeated usage, wind and varmints, and attractive. The main ingredients in the pen are boards, chicken wire, polypropylene tarpaulin and nail, screws or bolts to hold it all together.

I use standard, kiln dried 2-inch framing lumber for the frame of the pen. These boards are readily available and with an annual coating of stain or wood preservative will last indefinitely. I don't use pressure treated lumber for the framing materials because of the negative environmental effects of the arsenic treating process. The chemicals used to pressure treat the lumber are toxic to humans, animals and plants, and create huge pollution problems at the pressure treating facility. The sawdust and fumes given off when you saw or burn pressure treated lumber are especially toxic. Do not breath these fumes.

Further, the lumber most often used for pressure treating is southern yellow pine that travels a long distance for use in my area. We have perfectly acceptable spruce and fir lumber in our region that doesn't require such polluting treatment or transport.

So far there doesn't appear to be any great advantage to using pressure treated lumber. The portable pens I built three years ago show absolutely no sign of deterioration.

Here's a list of materials and tools needed to construct the 4-foot by 10-foot chicken tractor. Note that typical "2x4" lumber actually measures only 1.5- by 3.5-inches. At the lumber yard check through the pile and reject any boards with splits, crooks or large knots. You will rip some of these boards in half length-wise, so you want the best boards you can get.

Ripping the framing members is much easier if you have a table or bench saw. It takes longer, but you can rip boards with a hand held power saw equipped with a ripping fence. Rip fences are available for most hand-held power saws. You can buy them at hardware stores or tool stores for less than $10.

Table 6: Materials and Tools You Need to Build a Chicken Tractor

- **Lumber**, kiln dried spruce or fir
  5 pieces 2- by 4-inch by 10 feet
  5 pieces 2- by 4-inch by 8 feet
- **Hinges**, 3 heavy duty piano type door hinges, 3-inches, galvanized steel (screws usually come in the hinge package)
- **Chicken wire**, 1-inch galvanized poultry netting, 28 feet of 36-inch width, and 10 feet of 48-inch width. Most hardware stores or farm supply stores will have these widths in stock and will cut them to length for you. Galvanized poultry wire will last several years. You can even buy PVC coated wires that will last virtually forever, although it is more expensive.
- **Screws**, 100, 3-inch galvanized, and 100, 1.5-inch galvanized
- **Staples**, 1-pound, 1-inch galvanized poultry staples
- **Tarpaulin**, 8-feet x 16-feet, polypropylene
- **Laths**, 1/4-inch by 1.5-inch x 4-feet, need 16 pieces ripped from 2x4 lumber, or use pre-made lath strips from the lumber yard.
- **Hasp lock with keeper** to hold the lid closed.
- **Scissors or sharp knife** to cut tarp.
- **Saw** - hand or power
- **Hammer**
- **Drill** with screwdriver head
- **Framing square** or speed square
- **Staple gun** and staples
- **C-clamps**, pipe clamps or furniture clamps
- **Tape measure**
- **Wire cutting pliers** or shears

Use a saw to cross cut the boards to the proper length. Saw-horses and c-clamps make the task of ripping boards easier. You can also use over-turned buckets or milk crates to support the work while you are sawing. A ripping blade or a combination rip and crosscut blade will work fine to do the cutting. Of course, the ripping goes much easier if you have a table saw.

A 16-ounce carpenter's hammer is all you need to drive in the staples. You can also use it to start screws in the soft wood, then use the power drill or screwdriver to drive the screws tight.

Use C-clamps or furniture clamps to hold runners and braces in place while you are screwing them tight. The best way to achieve structural rigidity is to have square end cuts and tight screws. Once the frame is erect, the cross braces combined with the poultry wire and poly tarp will serve to further reinforce the structural integrity of the frame.

Use 2- by 4-inch boards to frame the bottom runners on both sides and the ends. They strengthen the frame and resist decay. Make the 2-by 2-inch framing members by ripping 2- by 4-inch boards in half lengthwise. This makes the unit lighter while still maintaining structural rigidity.

If you lack carpentry skills it may be best to ask a friendly neighbor to give you a hand, at least with the first frame. It's not important to create a masterpiece of architecture and carpentry, but it is necessary to create a frame that will withstand continuous moves, heavy winds and snows, and any varmints that might try to break in.

The job of pen construction is certainly possible by yourself, but it will go much easier and faster if you have a helper to hold pieces in place for sawing and assembling.

Step 1: After all your materials and tools are on site, you can begin the task of building the chicken tractor by ripping the 2x4 boards to make the 2x2 runners, end braces and lid frame and braces. You need to make:

- six pieces of 2x2-10 feet long
- eight pieces of 2x2-45 inches long
- four pieces of 2x2-36 inches long
- two pieces of 2x2-48 inches long
- one piece of 2x2-36 inches long for lid prop
- save extra pieces for corner braces, cut ends to 45 degrees.

After all your boards are ready, you can stain them with a fast drying exterior grade wood preservative. This will add years to the life of your pen and will make it more attractive.

Step 2: After the stain or wood preservative has dried sufficiently, start assembling your pen. On a level surface such as a garage floor or driveway, lay out your first side. Place a 10-foot 2x4 laying flat. This is the bottom runner of the first side.

Then place a 2x2x36 piece at each end, on the outside of the long pieces, to form a 90 degree angle. Lay a 2x2x10-feet piece across the top and a 2x2x10-feet piece in the middle. The assembled pieces resemble a "gate" lying on the ground.

Step 3: Use the carpenter's square to make sure that each corner is exactly 90 degrees. This is important throughout the project to ensure a square, level and plumb structure that is rigid and stable.

Another way to check for square is to use the 3-4-5 technique. Measure down one end 3 feet (a) and along the side 4 feet (b). The diagonal (c) should be exactly 5 feet. If it isn't, just scoot the frame one way or the other to make the measurements come out correctly (see diagram).

Figure 11: Checking Square

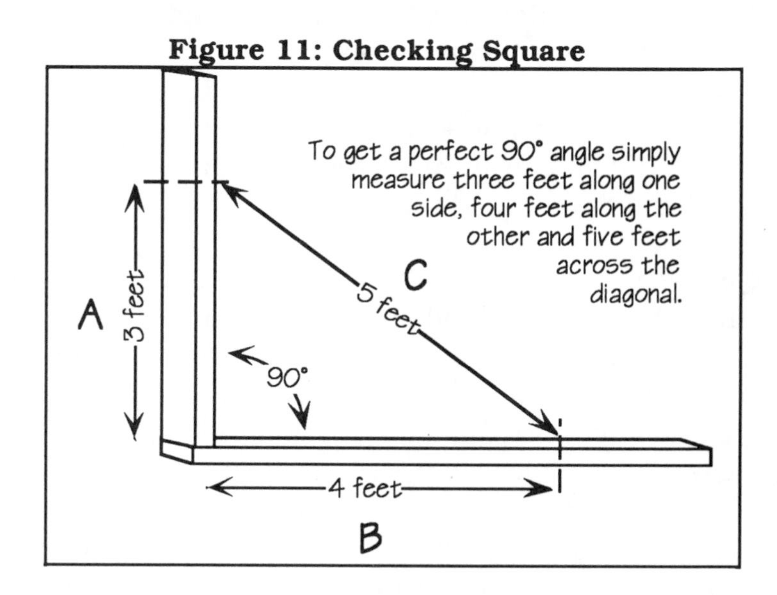

Step 4: Use the 3-inch galvanized screws and the screwdriver to attach the framing members to each other. Use two screws at each end of the 2x4 bottom board, and 2 screws at each end of the middle brace and top board. You can use a hand screwdriver for this task, but it is much easier and faster with a power drill or power screwdriver. Re-check the frame for square, then tighten all screws securely. It is certainly faster to nail the frame, but the screws will hold tighter and last longer.

Step 5: Set the first side out of your way and build the second side, following steps 1 through 4.

Step 6: Set the two side panels upright, making sure the 2x4 bottom boards are at the bottom. Space the side panels parallel and 45-inches apart.

Step 7: Have your helper hold the side panels upright while you install the end braces. Install the following:

2x4x45-inch bottom end brace at each end
2x2x45-inch middle end brace at each end
2x2x45-inch upper brace at each end.

Continually check for square as you screw the end braces in place with 3-inch galvanized screws, with at least 2 screw in each 2x4 and 2 screws in each 2x2.

Step 8: Now install two 2x2x45-inch cross braces between the upper braces of the side panels, measuring in 42 inches from each end. These braces will provide lateral stability and a place to hang your waterer and feeder. Install braces on each side to support the load of the cross braces that hold up the waterer and feeder.

Step 9 (optional): If you are building your chicken tractor for laying hens you will want to install two 2x2x45-inch roosts between the middle braces of the side panels, measuring in 14 inches from each end of the pen. These roosts provide roosting space for 10 or 12 hens. Half of them will be at each end of the pen. This will help distribute the manure evenly and will lessen crowding. See chapter 14 for design specifications of roosts. You also need nest boxes in one end of the pen. Three nests will be plenty for 10 or 12 hens. Make the nests about 14-inches wide by 14-inches high by 14-inches deep. You can install them next to the lid so that the eggs are easy to pick by simply raising the lid.

You now have a boxed frame that should be square and level, and ready for installing the chicken wire on all four sides, and the tarpaulin on the back side and both ends.

Step 10: To install the 36-inch chicken wire, lay the frame on its side. Have your helper hold the chicken wire in place while you nail it securely with 1-inch galvanized poultry staples every 8 to 12 inches. Be sure to square the chicken wire with the pen so that you can get a continuous wrap around all four sides. This will insure stability, and it's easier and faster to install if you don't have to cut the wire in sections to get it square on the frame. A tip: use the staple gun to hold the wire in place until you get it nailed securely with the 1-inch poultry staples.

After installing the wire on the first side, roll the wire around the end and flip the frame to its other side. This is much easier to do if you have a helper. Then, continue stretching the wire around the frame and securing it with poultry staples.

Step 11: To install the poly tarp, lay the frame on its front side. Cut the tarp to fit the back panel that now measures 36 inches by 10 feet 3 inches. Hold the tarp in place, making sure it covers the side squarely. Use the staple gun to hold the tarp in place temporarily. Then, using the 1/4 lath boards and the 1-1/2 inch galvanized screws, install a lath board over each framing member, held in place with a short screw every 12 inches. These lath boards will hold the tarp in place, keeping the wind or varmints from ripping it. Install tarp on both ends of the pen and secure it with lath strips.

Step 12: Now, set your nearly finished chicken tractor upright, check it for square, and get ready to build and install the lid.

Step 13: To build the lid, lay out the 2x2x10 framing members parallel on your work surface 45 inches apart. At each end install a 2x2x48-inch end brace. Measure in 42 inches from each end and install a 2x2x45-inch cross brace. Check the lid frame for square, screw the pieces together and place it on your chicken tractor.

Step 14: Install the hinges along the back side of the lid and attach them to the upper brace of the rear wall. Place the hinges 12 inches from each end, with one in the middle of the lid. Then, install the latch in the middle of the front of the lid, with the latch keeper mounted on the upper brace of the front wall.

Use a good quality latch with a positive lock mechanism. This will keep heavy winds from shaking the latch loose. This happened to my second generation pen. The lock hasp failed and the hinges broke when the lid blew off backwards in a strong wind.

Step 15: You are now ready to install the 48-inch poultry wire on the lid of your chicken tractor. Use the same technique you did in installing the wire on the sides and end of the pen. Then finish off the job by installing the poly tarp on the lid. Make sure to leave a 1/2-inch gap between the ends of the laths on the lid, so rain water can find its way off without excessive pooling.

Step 16: Install a 1.5- by 1.5-inch by 3-foot stick to prop the lid open while you are taking care of the chickens—similar to the hood prop in your car. Mount this on a center brace, with a keeper hook on the end to hold it in place while the lid is open, and to store it when you close the lid. Hold the prop in place with a screw through the cross member, and attached to the lid frame with a hook and eye screw. This will prevent knocking the lid loose while you are inside the pen and having it fall on you. It will also prevent the wind from catching it and blowing it backwards off the pen.

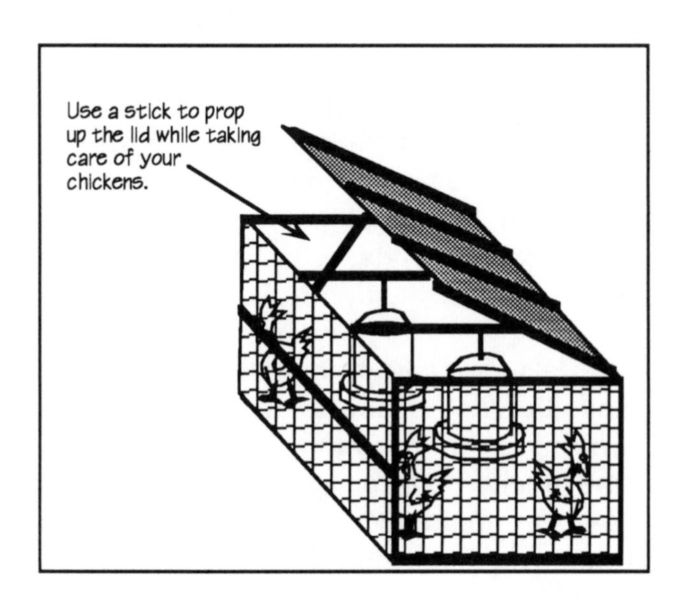

Step 17 (optional): It's much easier to apply stain or wood preservative to the boards before assembling them, but in some cases I've left the staining until the last step before I install the poly tarp. Having done it both ways, I now feel it makes more sense to stain the boards first, then touch up any scratches or bare spots after assembling the pen. Be sure to stain the lath strips, too, to protect them from weather and to make them look better. I use a "cedar" colored stain that is very attractive. Your pen is now complete and ready to use.

To use your chicken tractor frame as a cold frame or growing tunnel, you should screw the lath boards that hold the poly tarp rather than use staples. Then, when you want to take the tarp off to install greenhouse film it's a simple matter to unscrew the laths to make the change over.

You can use the same construction sequence and building techniques for creating whatever size pen you choose to make. It costs about $75 to build a 4-x10-foot chicken tractor that will hold 20 broilers or 10 laying hens if you use all new materials. It will cost 3 times that much to build a 10-x12-foot pen, but the larger pen will hold 4 times as many chickens. The per bird cost is lower in the larger pen. If you plan to grow a large number of birds on open range, this bigger pen can make a difference. You can decide which size pen suits your needs after you've developed your business plan.

Use any materials you have on hand to build these pens, and the materials I've listed above are ones that are readily available in my area at fairly low cost. In developing countries the chicken tractor system will work wonderfully, except for one circumstance. Oftentimes, there is no access to chicken wire and dimension lumber to build the pens.

In this event substitute native materials such as bamboo poles for framing, bamboo shoots and other types of vines for weaving the fence, and fronds from trees such as palms to provide cover from rain and sun.

3. Using the Chicken Tractor

By using narrow framing members and light sheathing, the pen is light enough for one person to move, yet heavy enough to resist wind, varmints and repeated usage. To move the pen just pick up one end and drag it slowly as the chickens walk along inside. For a larger pen you may need a helper to lift the other end and help scoot the pen forward.

Without a helper the best way to move the larger 10-foot by 12-foot pen is to place a set of wheels such as a furniture dolly under one end, then walk to the other end of the pen and pull it where you want it. Poultry grower Mike Yoder in Pennsylvania had his welder friend make up a yoke with lawnmower wheels on it for $18.

It's even simpler and less expensive to use wooden scoots. Cut these out of two 2x4 boards into a half-moon shape. Cut a notch in the top of the scoot board so the bottom end runner of the pen can fit in. This holds the scoot in place while you are moving the pen.

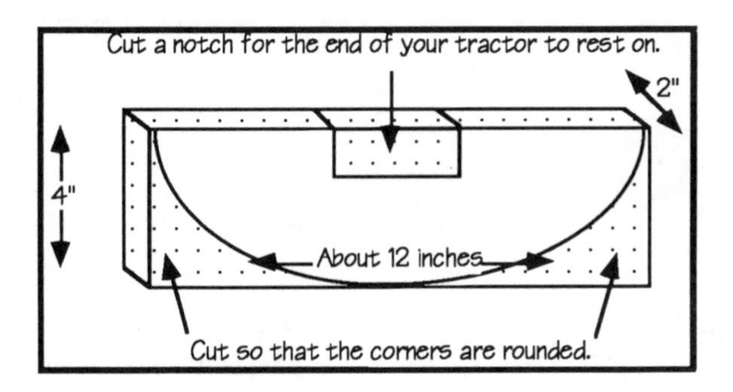

Figure 12: How to Scoot Your Tractor

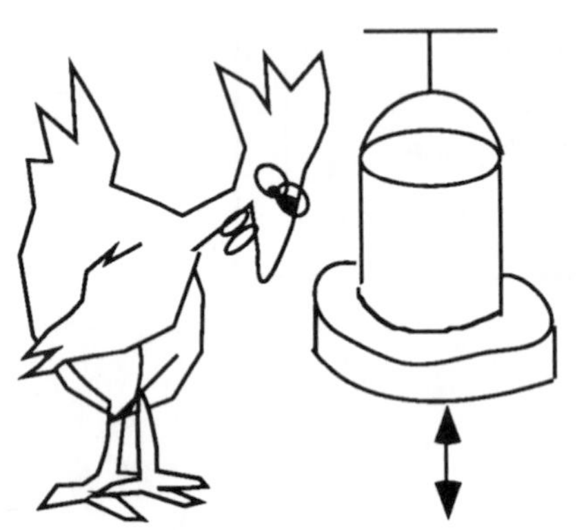

Suspend water and food containers about chicken chest high to keep them cleaner.

Hang the waterer and feeder from the cross brace under the roof. Arrange it so you can raise the buckets as the chickens get larger, keeping the lip of the feeder tray about chest high on the birds. This will help keep much of the feces and dust out of the water and feed, and make it harder for them to waste feed by brushing it out as they eat. They have a habit of tilting their heads sideways as they peck, and raking food out onto the floor.

Chapter 4: Selecting Chickens for Your Tractor

Breeds to Choose From and Best Choices

There are many more breeds of chickens to choose from than you will ever need. One current breeder catalog—Murray McMurray Hatchery—lists 10 layer breeds, 30 different bantam breeds, 30 dual purpose breeds and 4 meat breeds. They also list over 30 show breeds, as well as partridge, pheasants, turkeys, ducks and geese. Another breeder, Marti's Poultry Farm, lists 60 different chicken breeds, many of them old line heritage breeds. (see appendix for addresses).

Your choice depends entirely on which breeds intrigue you, and whether you want meat, eggs or show birds. Buy layers if you simply want eggs. Buy meat birds if you only want meat. If you want both, then consider buying a standard dual purpose breed such as Plymouth Barred Rock. You get eggs or fryers from the females and fryers or broilers from the males.

If you want fast growing meat birds for market, choose one of the hybrid meat varieties such as Cornish Cross, Kosher King or Silver Barred Cross. These hybrids have a high rate of feed conversion and are fast growers. Any hybrid's offspring will be throwbacks to the original parents and will likely be worthless for either meat or egg production. If you want to keep a rooster for fertile eggs, you will need to keep the standard breeds.

One factor that is most important to the chicken tractor garden is the foraging characteristics of the breed you choose. All the standard breeds will be aggressive foragers, eating bugs, weeds, grasses and worms. Their ability to forage for food helps save a great deal of grain you would otherwise have to buy.

On the other hand, the hybrids, particularly the high maintenance hybrid meat birds will be very poor foragers, preferring to get their food from the feed bucket. My experience corresponds to the experience of other growers who say that their hybrid meat birds won't even go outside the coop to walk about or graze. They are just too lazy.

For the chicken tractor farmer I'd recommend you stick with the standard breeds. Especially the old line breeds that are in danger of becoming extinct such as those listed in the following chapter.

Many of the old line standard breeds are only available from small local hatcheries. I think we should all do what we can to keep the independent hatcheries in business. Most of them are family owned and operated and are carrying on a lineage of service to their customers that has been in their families for decades, even generations.

These hatcheries also have a tremendous amount of information at their fingertips and can help you over the rough spots with your poultry problems; especially disease and nutrition questions. If we don't support these hatcheries, then another part of our country's heritage will eventually fade from the scene and we will lose many of the old line poultry breeds forever.

One of the most satisfying aspects of raising your own poultry, for meat, eggs or show, is that you can breed your own hens. Just put a rooster in with the hens, gather the eggs and hatch them. By doing this year after year you will improve your flock. You can even create a new strain, based on your own criteria and specific needs.

Following is a partial list of the commercial breeds that are readily available through feed stores and mail order catalogs. This is not a complete list. Instead, these are varieties that are available from commercial breeders and that have proven to be capable of performing well for their purpose.

Words really can't describe the beauty and presence of these distinctly different breeds of chickens. My primary hope in including this list is simply to give you an idea of the enormous number of poultry breeds available for meat or eggs, for dual purpose and for show or exhibition. There is a separate listing of turkeys, partridge, pheasants, ducks and geese in Chapter 15, along with a list of rare breeds published by The American Livestock Breeds Conservancy.

Table 7: Breeds available from commercial hatcheries

Bantams	
Light Brahma	Pure white with black laced tail and hackle feather
Buff Brahma	Golden buff with black tails and laced hackles
Dark Brahma	Silver Penciled greenish black base and silvery white on neck, saddle and tail
Silkes	Available in buff, black, white and blue
Booted Bantams	Bearded and non-bearded
Mille Fleur	Reddish bay feathers tipped in white
Porcelain	Pale blue tipped in white
Sultan	Features beard and muffs, feathered legs and 5 toes
Cochin Bantams	Buff, partridge, red, barred, black with green sheen, golden laced, red, white, black, mottled & blue
Gold and Silver Sebrights	Golden bay and Silver white
Japanese	Black, buff, and white with black tail
Old English Games	Very cocky
Quail Antwerp Belgian	Brownish black tinged with straw color.
White Laced Red Cornish	Clean legged variety
Silver Penciled Rock	Brown eggs, hatch well
Dark Cornish	Excellent to eat
Partridge Rock	Partridge color pattern
Partridge Wyandotte	For show, brown eggs or hobby
Rhode Island Red	Deep, mahogany color
White Crested Black Polish	Bright white top hat
Araucana Bantam	Lays colored eggs

Breeds available from commercial hatcheries (cont.)

Heavy Breeds	Brown egg layers, dual purpose-meat and eggs
Silver Laced Wyandottes	Hardy, vigorous, good winter layers, productive
White Orpingtons	Pure white, gentle, good layers
Buff Orpingtons	Glistening golden plumage, good layers and mothers and excellent to eat
Turkens	Naked necks, good layers and winter hardy, tasty .
Black Australorps	Australian heritage, good layers and table birds, gentle
Rhode Island Reds	Prolific layers, dual purpose
Red Star	Sex link, red females, white males, good layers, good to eat
New Hampshire Reds	Handsome and vigorous, good dual purpose birds
White Rocks	Good year round layers, fryers and roasters
Partridge Rocks	Excellent setters and brooders, eggs, meat or show
Barred Rocks	Dual purpose, America's favorite layer and roaster, reliable
Buff Rocks	Pure golden buff, fine winter layers and good setters
White Giants	Slow to mature heavy roaster, good egg layers
Black Giants	Exhibition, layer, table use, good cold weather variety, extra heavy at maturity
Speckled Sussex	Beautiful utility bird, for showing, eggs or table
Dark Cornish	Superb meat qualities and hardy foragers
White Wyandottes	Snow white plumage, ideal for table, early to finish, good for northern climates, good layers, wonderful dual purpose bird
Colombian Wyandottes	Medium size birds, good layers, setters and brooders
Light Brahmas	Old Asian breed, gentle, cold hardy, good layers, slow to maturity roasters, fine quality meat
Columbian Rocks	Black on white, very nice for show

Breeds available from commercial hatcheries (cont.)

White Egg Layers	
Blue Andalusians	Spanish origin, blue-laced plumage, not good brooders, excellent for exhibition and fly tying
Silver Spangled Hamburgs	Small size, alert, graceful, elegant and beautiful, great foragers, easy keepers
Red Leghorns	Rare show hen, not good setters, rich red plumage, graceful
Anconas	Excellent layers, lustrous black plumage with white tips, old Mediterranean breed.
Single Comb Brown Leghorns	Colorful, chicks are striped like chipmunks, lively, good layers, non-setters
Rose Comb Brown Leghorns	Rose combs are low, solid, thick, and covered with small rounded points, less likely to suffer frostbite, good range bird
Black Minorcas	Large Mediterranean, large eggs, non-setters
Buff Minorcas	Rich, golden buff color, large eggs, non-setters
Araucanas	"Easter Egg Chicken", Chilean, medium size, extremely hardy, eggs colored turquoise to deep olive
Pear White Leghorn	Prolific, long lived hybrid, good feed to eggs conversion, hardy, out performs most standard breeds
Highland 55	Hybrid cross between heavy breed males and large White Leghorn females, hardy, prolific egg layer

Breeds available from commercial hatcheries (cont.)

Crested Breeds	White egg layers, ancient breeds from Poland
White Crested Black Polish	Black plumage, white crest
Golden Polish	Ornamental, very showy,
Buff Laced Polish	Golden buff laced with creamy white. Showy, gentle, both bearded and non-bearded
White Polish	Snowy white crests and rounded white bodies look like snowballs. Dainty and pretty
Silver Polish	Striking appearance, non-setters
Sultans	Southeastern Europe origin, crest, muff, beard, feathered shanks and five toes
Crevecoeurs	Normandy France origin, all black plumage, lays white eggs
Mottled Houdans	France origin, lovely black plumage tipped with white, 5 toes, delicious eating and good layers
Cochins	
Black Cochins	Coal-black, exhibition
White Cochins	Giant snowballs, quiet
Buff Cochins	Poor layers but great setters
Partridge Cochins	Orange-red, show and setting
Blue Cochins	Rare and beautiful
Silver Laced Cochins	Silver laced plumage
Feather footed breeds	
White Langshan	Stately, white plumage, brown eggs, showy
Black Langshan	Asiatic, large, glossy black, gentle, showy, brown eggs
Dark Brahmas	Striking, gentle, silver penciled gray and black with silvery white
Buff Brahmas	Large, gentle, regal, brown eggs, showy, will set
Salmon Faverolles	France origin, novelty, showy, large sized

Breeds available from commercial hatcheries (cont.)

Rare and Unusual Breeds	
Silver Gray Dorkings	Ancient Rome, long body on short legs
Sumatras	Island of Sumatra, Asia, long tailed, beautiful
Golden Penciled Hamburgs	Fine, small, active, white eggs, non-setter
White Laced Red Cornish	Handsome, blocky Cornish, slow to mature
Phoenix	Imperial gardens of Japan, long tail feathers
Lakenvelders	Germany and Holland, small, quick, active
Buttercups	Sicily, excellent for show
White Faced Black Spanish	Graceful and stylish, slow to develop, oldest of the Mediterranean's
Golden Campines	Belgium, small, distinctive
Red Caps	English, large rose comb
Silver Leghorns	Silvery white and lustrous black, good layers and very vigorous, outstanding show
Golden laced Wyandottes	Formerly called "Winnebagoes", showy
Dominiques	American, also called "Dominiker", very hardy, good layers
Silver Penciled Rocks	Exhibition, ideal fly tying feathers, single comb
Silver Penciled Wyandottes	Showy, fly tying, rose comb
Egyptian Fayoumis	Small, active, Nile in Egypt, quick to mature as layers and broilers

Breeds available from commercial hatcheries (cont.)

Meat Birds	**Hybrid crosses**
Cornish Game Hen	Harvest at 2.5 pounds live weight for delicious eating
Jumbo Cornish X Rocks	Rapid growth, feed efficient, dress from 3 to 4 pounds in 6 to 8 weeks, pullets take 1 to 1.5 weeks longer to reach maturity for slaughter, not good foragers
Cornish Roaster	Fryer or roaster, slower maturing, fewer leg problems, more active than Cornish Cross, better forager, dress at 3-4 pounds in 8-9 weeks.

Excerpted with permission from Murray McMurray Hatchery catalog

Chapter 5: Give Me That Old Time Chicken

...and It's Good Enough for Me

Stepping Backwards Into The Future

Since time began, poultry, and especially chickens, have provided food and valuable products for humanity. However, new technology including: refrigeration, transportation, large brooders and incubators, trade associations and contract growers have changed the way we think about and raise chickens.

The industrial meat and egg factories have resulted in a drastic decline in the farm flocks and small hatcheries. Independent hatcheries have closed by the hundreds across America, paralleling the alarming decline in farm flocks and farm families.

Current industry standards favor hybrid crosses over pure breeds. It's true that per bird production in both eggs and meat has increased, while feed consumption per bird has dropped. It's just as true that flavor, nutrition, disease resistance, foraging abilities and weather hardiness have also declined. Consumers have to settle for bland, flavorless--often contaminated—produce from the supermarkets. To get good tasting poultry we have to grow it ourselves or buy it from a nearby farmer who still practices humane, sustainable livestock husbandry.

According to the American Livestock Breeds Conservancy, there are about nine companies that control the breeding stock for all commercial meat and egg chickens in North America. Did you know that we currently have endangered breeds of livestock in just the same way we have endangered wild life? As with other animals and plants in the world, some breeds of chickens are at risk of extinction and we are rapidly losing genetic diversity.

Hybrid industrial breeds, designed for commercial production, are very fragile. They require antibiotics in feeds, and extra management to prevent diseases. They require a high protein diet and they suffer in confined housing. This housing requires a tremendous amount of energy for heating and cooling. So what if the new hybrid freaks can out-produce the old heritage breeds? They are doing so at great harm to our environment. Grain farms are in one region and broiler houses are in another. This requires a tremendous amount of long distance trucking. The broiler and layer factories themselves are in states with low wages and lenient pollution laws. Worst of all, the new hybrid breeds just aren't "real" chickens.

Howard W. "Bud" Kerr, Jr., Director of the Office for Small-Scale Agriculture at the USDA, told me a story about trying to use free range chickens for pest control in his peach orchard. He got some hybrid broilers from a commercial breed, but, when he put his portable pen in the orchard, they would not go outside! The only thing these ultra-hybrid birds know how to do is gain weight quickly in protected confinement housing with continuous feeding.

I'm not saying you can't raise the high energy hybrids if you want to, but the chicken tractor system works best with "real" chickens. The standard breeds are aggressive foragers. They withstand changing weather better than the hybrids and they taste better. You just cannot deny the lower fat, better flavor and healthier texture of the old line breeds. Just like your grandmother used to cook, hmmm gooood!

Also, the old line breeds of chickens display physical characteristics and personality traits more than the new hybrid breeds.

Today, changing global economic conditions and trade agreements are affecting almost every individual somehow. Our climates are shifting. I don't know of a single country that has not had unusual weather in the last several years. We need these hearty older breeds and we need to actively preserve them. I support the American Livestock Breeds Conservancy (ALBC) for their efforts in saving the endangered farm breeds and I encourage you to contact them to find out more about their programs and rescue efforts. The best place you can begin to preserve the past, for a brighter future is in your garden—with old time breeds.

"*Most of these older breeds, besides being productively versatile, are also beautiful! They have a satisfying aesthetic value that alone merits their keeping and gives joy just to have them around.*" Donald Bixby, DVM, American Livestock Breeds Conservancy

Preserving Heirloom Poultry Breeds

by Donald Bixby, DVM
Executive Director of the American Livestock Breeds Conservancy

Chickens and other poultry were some of our first domesticated animals. They have provided a widely adaptable food source used by almost every culture. Poultry have been effective foragers living on the scraps of human activity and providing meat, eggs, feathers, down, and pest control. Explorers and settlers carried them everywhere to provide a portable source of fresh meat and to establish flocks at pioneer farms. There was once a time when chicken flocks were on every farm as well as in most back gardens of town and city dwellers. These poultry flocks were profitable for small farms and regional hatcheries, too.

Along with utility, people have always recognized and appreciated the beauty of poultry. A tremendous variety of type, shape, size, color, and feather pattern and comb are available. The skills of breed selection, whether for production or perfection of form, have been widespread historically.

Some Breeds Face Extinction

Following World War II there was a major restructuring of egg and poultry production. Meat and egg production are completely industrialized, resulting in a drastic decline in the farm flocks and small hatcheries. Today, poultry is big business; produced in factory farms, not on family farms. Industrialization has made poultry meat and eggs an inexpensive source of protein. Unfortunately, while poultry consumption is at an all time high, consolidation of the poultry industry has led to a loss of breeds, genetic diversity, and the widespread knowledge of selection skills.

Genetic selection limited to a few uniform production characteristics with little regard to innate hardiness has led to the decline of the many formerly important breeds. The industry favors hybrid crosses over pure breeds and vertical integration has resulted in fewer people making decisions about breed selection. The result is a very narrow genetic base controlled internationally by only a few companies. Although existing industrial stocks may be suitable for commercial production, they don't do well in less closely controlled conditions. In return for its high productivity, industry produced poultry requires a high level of input, including substantial veterinary attention, high protein feed and confinement housing.

As breeds disappear, valuable traits—developed over many generations—are also being lost. Researchers at Rodale Farms hoped to use chickens as biological control of plum curcullio in their apple orchard. Hatchery hybrids would not even go outside their hen house let alone forage for the pest larvae in the orchard. The valuable traits of foraging and ranging have been bred out! The American Livestock Breeds Conservancy suggested Dominique chickens, American's oldest recognized poultry breed, long noted for its foraging ability. Sure enough, the Dominiques were in chicken heaven scratching and pecking through the orchard debris and foraging insect larvae as well as other morsels tasty only to chickens.

The American Livestock Breeds Conservancy

The American Livestock Breeds Conservancy (ALBC) has been helping to conserve heritage breeds since 1977. We have an active program to conserve the genetic pool for poultry, asses, cattle, goats, horses, sheep and swine. Many of the traits necessary for survival are not being passed along in the breeding programs of commercial poultry. Specifically bred out are the abilities to brood chicks, forage, produce both meat and eggs and adapt to climate changes.

The chicken tractor approach fits the small flock grower and hobbyist very well and provides a "habitat" for endangered poultry breeds. These breeds possess the very traits needed for the chickens to forage and thrive out-of-doors. This means we should consider them superior to the commercial hybrids for your garden. Besides being versatile, the heritage breeds are also beautiful. They have a satisfying aesthetic value that alone merits their keeping and gives me joy just to have them around.

> "*To safeguard our future, we cannot afford to let go of our valuable poultry heritage and the irreplaceable variety of breeds it represents.*" 1987 ALBC Poultry Census and Source Book.

Today there is a growing emphasis on sustainable agriculture that includes locally grown food and humanely raised livestock. Consumers want to know who produces their food, where, and under what conditions. Additionally, changing global economic conditions and trade agreements are affecting almost every individual in some way. There is widespread concern about climate changes and the continued availability of cheap energy. All of these issues affect our ability to meet the agricultural needs of the future. Adaptation is only possible where alternatives have been conserved. Genetic diversity provides these alternatives to selection of livestock to meet changing needs.

To encourage and promote rare production breeds of poultry, ALBC conducts periodic updates about sources and the status of particular breeds and rescue efforts. ALBC can also give you information about breeds for maximum conservation of genetic diversity.

Poultry Census Summary

To assess the status of poultry genetic resources in the United States, the American Livestock Breeds Conservancy conducted a survey of 17 production breeds in 1987. Breeds included in the survey are of cultural, historical or economic significance in America. The survey distinguished between "production" and "exhibition" strains and limited its search for breeder sources of production bird to those listed in the US Department of Agriculture directory of participants in the 1986 and 1987 National Poultry Improvement Plan.

Categories of "rare", "minor", and "watch" reflect the size of the breeding population (the number of females in breeding flocks) and the number of sources of breeding flocks.

- **Rare**—Breeds with 500 or fewer females and fewer than three sources.
- **Minor**—Breeds with 2,000 or fewer females, and five or fewer sources, or a concentration of the breeding population in fewer than three sources.
- **Watch**—Breeds with 2,000 to 20,000 females, but fewer than ten sources, or a declining number of sources.

Table 8:Endangered Breeds of Poultry

Rare	Minor	Watch
Ancona	Black Jersey Giant	Barred Plymouth Rock
Black Minorca	Brown Leghorn	Black Australorp
Delaware	Khaki Campbell Duck	New Hampshire
Dominique		Rhode Island Red (old type)
White Jersey Giant		Rouen Duck
White Wyandotte		Toulouse Goose
Pilgrim Goose		
Bronze Turkey (unimproved)		

For more information about livestock conservation send a self-addressed stamped envelope to:

The American Livestock Breeds Conservancy
Box 477
Pittsboro, NC 27312
Phone (919) 542-5704

A copy of the complete 1987 ALBC *Poultry and Census and Source Book* is only $5.00.

Chapter 6: Raising Chicks

Where to Buy Chicks

The day the baby chicks arrive is always an exciting time for the poultry grower. They are so cute—little furry balls running about and chirping as if celebrating having survived the journey to your place.

You can order day old chicks through your local feed store, or from any of the hatcheries that advertise in magazines such as Organic Gardening, New Farm, Small Farms Today, The Natural Farmer and so forth. Other useful addresses and contacts are available from your state Department of Agriculture. They will have a packet of poultry information they will send to you on request, including hatcheries located in your state or region.

Generally, you need to place your order about 4 weeks ahead of the date you want the chicks to arrive. This gives the hatchery an idea of how many chicks they need to hatch to fill all their orders. You can also buy chicks from local feed or farm supply stores. Usually, feed stores place one order in late April or early May for both broilers and egg layers, and sometimes a second order in June for meat birds only. Feed stores often have several varieties for you to choose from. They will tell you what day to come and pick up your birds, and encourage you not to be late.

Whether you order them directly from the hatchery or from the feed store, the chicks will arrive by air freight or postal service. It's important that you go right away to pick them up. Just before they hatch, the baby chicks will ingest the remainder of the yolk in the egg. This only gives them enough nourishment to survive for up to 72 hours without food or drink. So, you need to get them unpacked and into your brooder quickly.

If you've ordered your chicks directly from a hatchery and they are being delivered by mail, the hatchery will notify you which morning to expect your birds at the post office. I've found it useful to let the post office know a few days in advance, and give them my phone number so they can call me the minute the chicks come in. That way there's very little delay in getting them unpacked and into the brooder where they can get fresh water and food.

The minimum order for mail delivery chicks is usually 25. Over the years hatcheries have found this is the optimum number to ship without losses to suffocation, freezing or other injury. Shippers use heavy duty cardboard boxes with air vent holes. The boxes can hold 100 chicks, with dividers to limit each section to 25.

If your chicks come through a feed store be sure to look through the chicks for any that are obviously sick, injured or undersized. Leave these with the store. It's easier for the store to get credit on the sick or dead birds than it is for you.

Feed stores will charge you maybe 10 cents per bird more than you will pay by ordering direct from the factory. That's okay, since the feed store takes the worry out of ordering and will be willing to help you pick out the needed accessories and feed, and will answer any questions you have.

Prices vary for chicks, from 40 cents per bird for popular breeds, up to $5.00 each for rare breeds. The meat birds I've bought recently cost 60 cents each if I specify all cockerels. The cockerels will usually grow out to about 1 pound more per bird than the hens on the same amount of feed and in the same amount of time. If you want all meat birds, the cockerels are definitely worth the extra 10 cent premium.

The hatchery staff will do the best they can to separate the hens from the cockerels, but you still may get one or two hens in with your batch of broilers. You probably won't notice this until about the 6th week when the hens aren't getting as large as the other birds, and their combs are much smaller and not as brilliantly colored.

It's okay to get a few hens mixed in with the cockerels. They dress out to a smaller weight and you can use them as fryers or for grilling. If you are selling meat birds some of your customers will ask for the smaller birds specifically.

One thing I have noticed is that during the seventh and eighth weeks the males will try to mount any females that are in the pen. This may cause a problem in confined areas. The mounting act is fairly rough and the hens may get injured. If they do, just separate the injured hen back to the nursery and let her recover. If it's close to harvest time anyway I just keep the hen in the nursery until it's time for the batch to go to the processor.

Roosters, Hatching Eggs and Broody Hens

If you want to hatch your own chicks you need a rooster to get fertilized eggs to hatch. If you let the rooster run with the hens you can assume he will keep all the hens bred, so any eggs you pick will most likely be fertile.

Eggs for hatching need to be less than 10 days old when you place them in the incubator or under a broody hen. They take 21 days to hatch.

Most of the newer breeds of laying hens have had most of the broodiness bred out of them. You will have better luck relying on one of the older standard breeds to do your setting and brooding for you.

If you have fertile eggs but no broody hens, just use an incubator. These are available for $100 or less from the larger mail order hatcheries. An incubator will last forever if you keep it clean and well maintained.

Incubating eggs is not difficult, and it can be a lot of fun, especially for children to see the miracle of birth take place. The incubator does need careful attention twice each day though, since the eggs need turning at twelve hour intervals so the embryo forms properly. The more sophisticated incubators have automatic egg turning which handles this chore for you. The moisture and temperature levels are important, too, to ensure optimal hatching results.

Generally, 50 to 85% of your fertile eggs will hatch. It's almost impossible to get 100% hatchability due to variations in temperature, humidity and fertility of eggs. Still, if you have your own breeding flock and pay $100 for an incubator you will be ahead of the game financially after hatching about 150 chickens.

Another advantage of the incubator is that it enables you to maintain your purebred flock, or even create your own strain by matching your best roosters to your best hens and hatching the off-spring.

At our place the first flight of birds arrives in early May and goes straight to the brooder. They are only one day old and very susceptible to a whole bunch of different diseases. Some birds become infected at the hatchery. Some of the diseases remain in the pens from one batch of birds to the next. It's important to clean cages and equipment carefully. Many of the poultry diseases transmit through fecal matter and dust. Put down fresh bedding for each new batch of chickens.

Commercial growers will probably wince when they hear this rather cavalier attitude towards chicken diseases. They regularly plan for at least a 5 percent loss, and sometimes suffer losses of 25 percent or more. The experience I've had, corroborated by many, many small-scale poultry growers across the country, is that very few birds die in these small home flocks. Nonetheless, you want to take every precaution you can to make sure that diseases don't spread from one batch to another.

After the first batch has moved to the chicken tractor it's time to think about ordering the next batch. Thanks to the warmer weather, the second batch will be in the brooder only two weeks, versus three weeks for the first batch. So, order your second batch to arrive two weeks before you harvest the first batch.

Then, as soon as you remove the first batch to the processing facility you can clean the chicken tractor and move the second batch from the brooder to the field. Following this schedule with your third and fourth batches will have your last batch of broilers finishing up by November 15. Then you can turn your attention to dressing your turkeys for Thanksgiving Day.

Table 9: Schedule for Multiple Batches of Chickens

May 1 to July 1 — first batch
June 15 to August 15 — second batch
August 1 to October 1 — third batch
September 15 to November 15 — fourth batch.

In warmer parts of the country you will be able to start your first batch on April 1 and finish out on December 1, for five full flights. This will extend your season, your work and your net profits, since you use the same facility for all five batches. In hotter climates it may not be practical to raise chickens during the heat of the summer.

If the weather is warm and sunny the chicks can go out to pasture as early as 7 days old. However, the first spring batch will probably need to be in the brooder for up to three weeks to get the chicks up to a size and strength where they can withstand the cooler outside temperatures and the damp days of spring.

Moving the two- or three-week old birds from the brooder to the chicken tractor is an easy matter for me. I spread hay in my pick-up truck camper cap. Then I load the chickens, close the cap lid and drive over to the chicken tractor for unloading.

If you don't have a barn, garage or basement for setting up your brooder you can use the chicken tractor itself. Just add extra tarps or covers and install a heat lamp. We use old cardboard boxes cut to strips and stapled or taped to the inside of the frame to round off the corners. This keeps the chicks from piling up in the corners. The cardboard is also a good shield against winds that might chill the young birds.

Equipment and Supplies You'll Need for Chicks

The equipment you'll need to raise baby chicks is neither expensive nor complicated. It consists simply of a circular enclosure about 3 feet in diameter to use as a brooder, a waterer, a feeder, heat lamp, wood shavings for bedding and a thermometer.

Figure 13: Brooder Equipment

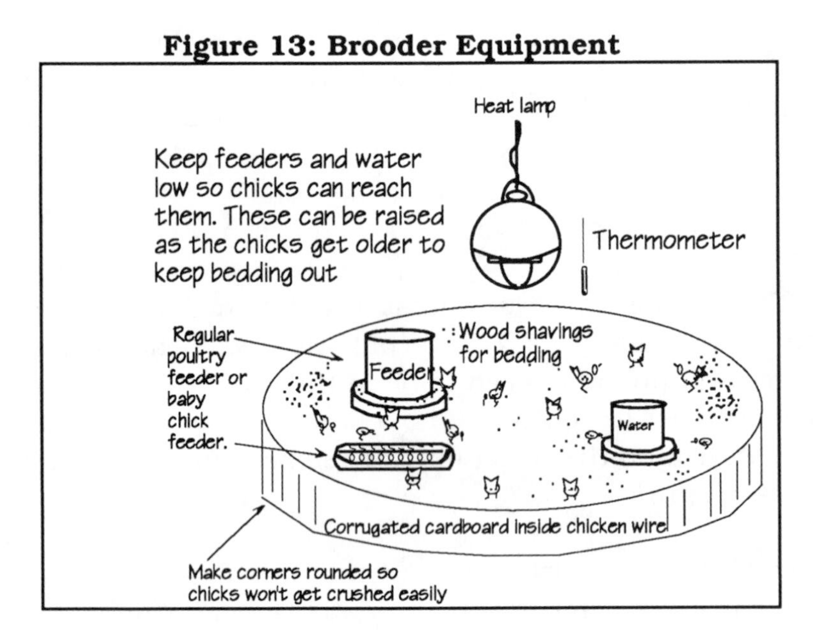

Brooder Space

The "brooder" is the place you keep the chicks from birth until they are old enough to go out to the shelter-pen. Generally, about 1/2 square foot per chick is enough space in the brooder. An enclosure about 3 feet in diameter gives plenty of room to brood 30 baby chicks. You will need a brooder area 5 to 6 feet in diameter for 50 chicks, and 100 chicks need about 7 to 8 feet diameter.

I make my brooder in a circular or oval shape using chicken wire with cardboard on the inside. The cardboard is at least 24 inches high and serves as a draft shield. Drafts can chill your chicks in no time, leading to sickness. You can tell when there is a draft in the brooder if the chicks huddle together against one side. The solution is to find where the draft is coming in and plug it with cardboard or some other draft-stopping material.

Figure 14: How to Tell if Your Brooder Has Drafts

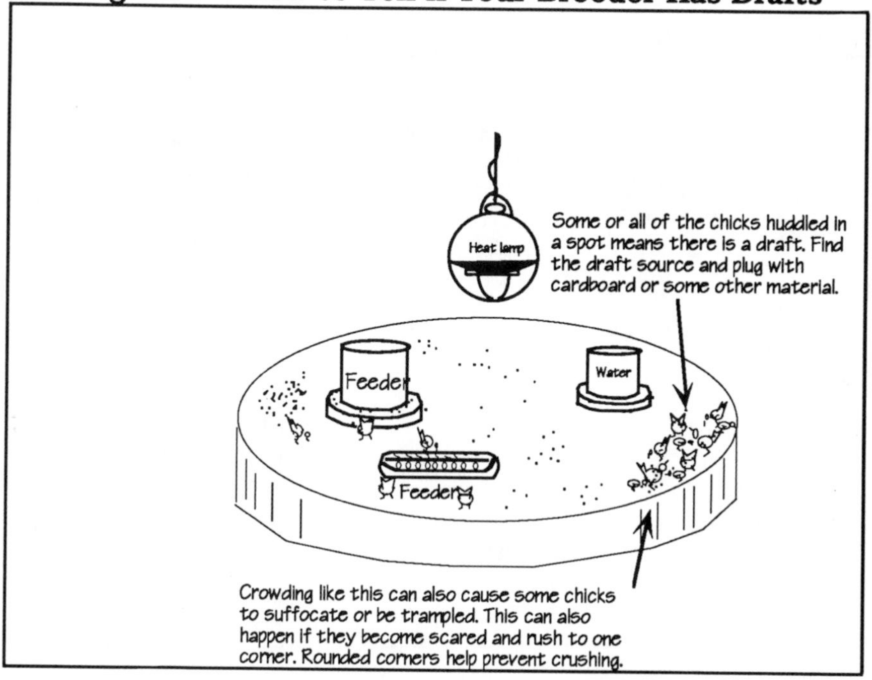

Light and Heat

Chicks need a temperature of about 90 to 95 degrees for the first week. Install a heat lamp over the center of the brooder cage. Red light bulbs are better than white ones because the chicks tend to peck at each other less under the red light. Fasten the lamp so you can raise or lower it as needed. If the chicks pile under the light they are too cold. Move the light closer to them or add a second lamp. They are too hot if they scatter to the edges of the pen or hide behind the waterer and feeder.

The area directly under the light should be 90 degrees F or a little higher for the first few days. The chicks will adjust their distance to the light to get a comfortable temperature. Make sure your brooder area is large enough for the chicks to move away from the heat lamp if they get too hot.

Figure 15: How to Tell if Chicks are Too Hot or Cold

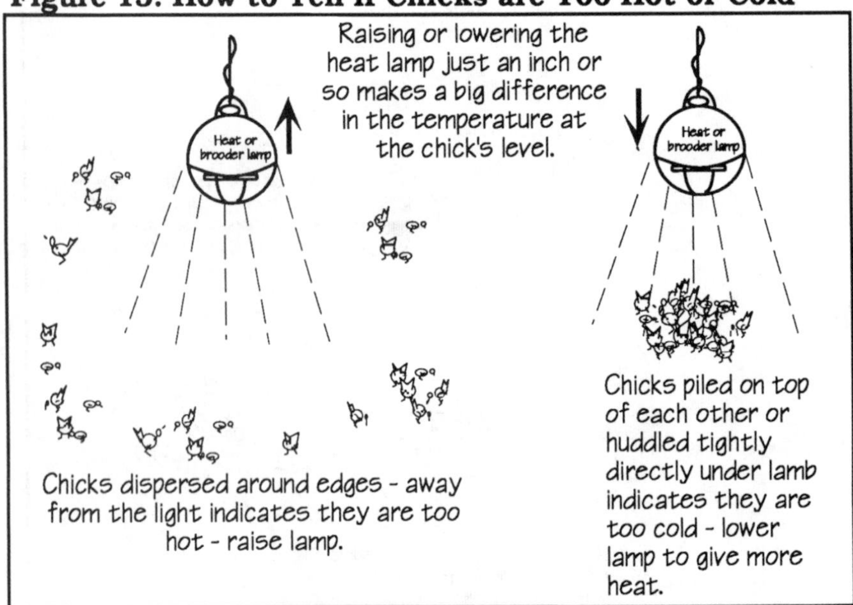

You can reduce the temperature about 5 to 10 degrees per week until they are comfortable at about 70 degrees. This gives them time to gradually acclimate to colder temperatures.

Water for Chicks

The chicks are only 1 or 2 days old when you pick them up at the farm store or when they arrive at the post office. Have at least 1 gallon of water for 50 birds. As you gently unpack them, dip the beak of each chick in the water before you turn it loose. They will be thirsty and dipping their beaks helps them find the water sooner. Most baby chick loss occurs because they don't start to eat or drink soon enough.

For the first day or two you can add about 3 tablespoons of sugar or honey to each quart of water to give them extra energy to recover from their trip. Never let your chicks run out of water—even after they are full grown. Chickens get dehydrated very quickly and can die before you know it. Always have fresh water available.

Chick Feed

Use a commercial chick starter mash for at least the first 2 weeks. If the chicks are having trouble recognizing the starter mash just cover the bedding near the feeders with newspaper and spread some feed on it. This will help them find the food. The newspaper will be needed for only about a day or so as they quickly learn to get food from the feeders.

Never feed lay ration to baby chickens. The extra calcium it contains for the egg layers can seriously injure the young chick's kidneys.

Have at least 2 feet of feeder space for 25 chicks. Some of the more timid chicks won't get enough to eat otherwise. Check them twice daily to keep the waterer and feeders clean and full. When the chicks move outside in the third week you can start feeding them grower pellets.

Grit for Chicks

All free ranging chickens will eat small pebbles or other grit to help digest their food in their gizzards. Grit that is available from the feed store is tiny insoluble granules of sand, stone or even shell. You can buy grit as limestone, oyster shells or granite. Most feed stores stock grit.

Even chicks need grit. Sprinkle it on their food. Do not sprinkle too much or they will fill up on the grit instead of food. When you are putting it on, think of it like salt; a little bit for seasoning. Do not feed baby chicks limestone grit. It contains calcium that will injure their kidneys.

Baby Bedding

Bedding can be any material that is dry, absorbent and dust free. I prefer wood shavings for bedding because it smells nice and absorbs urine, feces and spilled water quickly. However, you can also use straw, rice hulls, ground corn cobs or dry hay.

Sick or Injured Chicks

Listen to the chirp. Is it loud and shrill or perky and pleasant? Gail Damerow, in her delightful book *YOUR CHICKENS* says chickens make at least 30 different sounds. A sick chick will often tell you it doesn't feel well; both by the way it sounds and by its body language. Sometimes you might have some especially fragile chicks that need extra care. Bring these into the house and keep them in a cardboard box with a light bulb to keep them warm and unstressed until they recover.

Sometimes chicks get a touch of diarrhea and manure sticks to their rear ends. Too much protein in the feed can cause this. It is essential to remove this daily. Just gently pull it off. If it has hardened, I get a paper towel or cloth and warm water or olive oil to loosen it and gently wash it off. Pasted rears will disappear after a few days as the chicks grow and stabilize in their new home.

Chapter 7: Chicken Diet (Theirs, Not Ours)

In a natural setting—full of weeds and grasses, seeds, bugs, worms and so forth—chickens will be able to get an adequate diet. They will thrive on this diverse food intake, at least during the warmer months. Unfortunately, natural settings for chickens to forage are not always available.

Even if it's just on grass, intensive grazing in shelter-pens does give the chickens some access to a natural diet. However, the intensive grazing cannot meet all their dietary requirements. You need to supplement their diet with grain based chicken feed.

How much feed you will need depends entirely on the breed of chickens you're growing, the time of year, and whether you are growing layers, fryers or broilers. To grow the average meat bird to 4 pounds dressed weight will require from 12 to 15 pounds of grain feed.

A laying hen will require 18 to 20 pounds of feed from birth to egg laying age. Then she will require 80 to 90 pounds of grain feed per year. That seems like a lot of feed, I know, but not so much so when you compare it to one turkey that will eat nearly 80 pounds of feed to reach a market dressed weight of about 25 pounds.

Earlier I pointed out that it is possible to save as much as 30 percent on your feed bill by having the birds on pasture after they leave the brooder. According to Joel Salatin (see *Pastured Poultry Profit$*) you can insure the 30 percent savings by moving the flock to fresh graze daily. Make the move early in the morning and withhold grain for 1/2 to 1 hour. The grasses and weeds are most tender and most succulent early in the morning, and the birds are eager to begin morning feeding.

In an ordinary free range system in which the chickens just roam around the field the chickens have continual access to either grain feed or graze. They will fill up on grain, and use the grazing activity to stretch their legs and to satisfy their normal pecking and foraging instincts. In this case, the amount of grain feed saved can be as little as 10 percent. This foraging pattern was noted in several university tests, particularly at the Ohio and Vermont Agricultural Experiment Stations.

Even if your flock is only getting 10 percent of their nutritional requirements from graze and forage, this is probably the most important portion of their diet. The activity surrounding grazing and foraging is important for muscle tone and exercise. Sunlight is important for Vitamin D fixation.

The contact with the earth is important for access to small grit and the vitamins and enzymes in the soil. It also satisfies the bird's normal yearning for earth contact. The green plants themselves contain chlorophyll, a prime detoxifier that enables the birds to cleanse their digestive systems regularly. All of these combine to make a better tasting, healthier poultry.

Some grasses and weeds are better for grazing poultry than others. In a more natural setting, it is best to allow chickens to have access to as many varieties of plants as possible. Some plants are higher in protein, while others are higher in carbohydrates and so forth.

Given its choice, the chicken will eat the plants that provide the best diet for its needs. With a diverse variety of grasses, legumes, weeds and herbaceous forbs, the chickens will have access to what they need when they need it. This forage diversity leads to a more sustainable diet for the chickens.

Organic Feeds

My experience convinces me that chickens will excel when grown on organic feeds. Given free choice of organic versus conventionally grown grains, the chickens will become very adept at selecting the organic grains first. They will gain weight faster, have a better quality of meat, and will taste superior to the chickens raised on conventional grain. This is only my opinion, of course. To my knowledge professional research has neither proven nor disproven my position.

Taste is a very subjective thing, with each of us having a particular sense of what tastes good and what doesn't. Chickens have this innate sense of healthy food compared to not-so-healthy food. It is not uncommon to have organically fed chickens gain weight faster by about 10 percent, on about 10 percent less organic feed than conventionally grown chickens.

The problem, of course, is finding affordable organic feed for your chickens. It simply may not be available in your area. If it is available it may be inordinately expensive. In any case, you can use conventional feed grains and still expect reasonable gains and the flavor will still be superior to the poultry you would otherwise buy in the supermarket.

If you have land and time available, it may be worth your while to grow grain and hay for your chickens. If you don't have land and time, consider starting or joining an organic grain cooperative. These cooperatives are buying in grain from nearby farmers in bulk and repacking it for distribution to the cooperative members.

Reasons for growing organic grains or starting an organic grain cooperative are:

1. Healthier animals

2. Better tasting eggs and meat

3. Faster weight gains

4. Providing a market for organic grain growers to help them stay in business and to encourage more farmers to convert to organics

If you are growing a large number of poultry, you might be able to get your local feed mill to grind your feed for you. Usually this service is only available for quantities of two tons or more at a time. If you are part of a grain cooperative, you can split the order among the members to accommodate the needs of the feed mill.

When mixing your own feed ration, even if you're feeding organic grains, you will want to add a mineral package to the feed. A typical mineral package will contain Vitamins A, D, E, B-1, electrolytes and biotin. These mineral packages are available from mail order companies that sell poultry, production equipment and supplies.

Researcher H. R. Bird at the Ohio Agricultural Experiment Station found laying hens having access to good pasture can get 12 percent of the protein, 5 percent of the calcium, 100 percent of vitamins A and D, and 100 percent of the riboflavin necessary to sustain good egg production. Sunshine, of course, helps Vitamin D become available. This is a major contributor to the health and vigor of the pastured poultry flock.

It is possible—especially with the older breeds that are aggressive foragers—for the chickens to get many of their dietary needs from gleaning. In some scenarios, you can let the birds loose in the gardens for short periods of time to glean and control insect pests. I've found them especially helpful in controlling slugs in my mulched gardens.

Naturally, you want to let the hens have access to your garden only for a short time, and while you are there to keep an eye on them. It's also a good idea to turn them out in mature veggies instead of in the young succulent seedlings. Otherwise they'll ignore the slugs and wipe out your crops. In my experience, hens are particularly fond of ripe strawberries and ripe tomatoes.

Let the chickens into your garden in late afternoon and they will automatically go back to the pen at dusk. You won't have to chase them around to get them back in their pen. You can also train the chickens to follow you with a grain bucket. Thus, you can move them from pen to field and back a lot easier.

Another way to provide a diversified diet for your flock is to hand pick garden pests such as potato beetles and cabbage worms and feed them to the chickens. In areas where Japanese beetles are a problem in your garden your chickens will be a big asset in bug control. Expedite the collection process by hanging the beetle traps in the pen to attract bugs to the chickens.

If you don't have pasture available for your flock, you can feed good quality clover or alfalfa hay. What they don't eat will become bedding. The bedding will feed the soil microbes that help turn your chicken litter into rich compost. Chickens can also eat food preparation waste and table scraps. They will even eat meat scraps and peck at bones. They will particularly enjoy scraps of lettuce and other leafy greens from the household.

They Will Work for Chicken Feed

Your biggest expense in growing poultry will be feed, so let's look closely at the economics of chicken feed. You can buy chicken feed either as pellets or crumbled mash. There tends to be less waste with the pellets because the chickens have an eating habit of putting their beaks in the feed and tossing their heads spreading food all over. It is easier for them to peck wayward pellets off the ground than it is the crumbled feed.

I usually buy about 2 to 4 weeks worth of feed at a time rather than stock it too far ahead. It will get stale, especially in warmer weather. Feed also loses nutritional value as it gets older. Use up all the feed from one bag before you open another. Exposed to air, feed gets stale and can spoil.

I store the feed in a 30 gallon tin trash can and hold the lid on with a bungee cord. This is to prevent attracting rodents and wild birds to the feed. I prefer metal over plastic trash cans because the plastic tends to crack with extensive outdoor use—especially in cold weather.

Extra Treats

Chickens really like a variety of different feeds in their diet. You can feed your chickens many of the items you normally throw in your compost pile. They love leftover baked goods and vegetables, especially tomatoes and lettuce. Don't feed too many of the strong-tasting foods such as garlic, chives, onions or fish because these can make the eggs and meat taste odd.

Do not give your chickens anything that is rotten or spoiled. Your nose will tell you if the stuff should be compost or chicken feed. Chickens can get sick from eating rotten food.

You Can Grow Your Own Organic Feed

The amount of land you will need to grow grain for your flock depends on the climate, soil characteristics, cultural methods and your skill as a grower. Grain yields can range from as little as 2,000 pounds per acre up to 6,000 pounds per acre. At the lower yields you will need 1 acre of grain to feed 20 hens for a year. With increased soil fertility you can grow grain for 20 hens on just 1/3 acre.

It is possible however, to grow corn for scratch feed using any part of your garden or field that doesn't have other food crops on it. Because corn is easier to handle than the other grains, you might find it enjoyable exercise to pick and shell ears and grind them in a hand grinder to make scratch feed.

In most commercial feed rations, corn makes up about 60 percent of the mix. Even on a small piece of land you can easily grow enough corn to lower your purchased grain costs. Harvesting corn is simple, just pull the ears off the stalks, peel back the husk and break it off the ear. Pitch the ear into a wheelbarrow, cart or pickup truck and deliver it to your storage bin.

To get the corn kernels off the cob requires either a hand sheller—which is fairly slow and laborious—or a mechanical sheller. You can buy mechanical shellers new or used for just a few hundred dollars. Grind the cobs in a hammermill type leaf and yard waste grinder and use them for bedding. You can grind the corn kernels in the hammermill, too. Use a fine screen in the grinder to break the kernels into small enough pieces for the chickens to eat. Mature layers can even eat whole corn.

Table 10: Some Reasons Why You Want to use Local Organic Grain

1. Providing a market for organic grain growers to encourage more farmers to convert to organic. Bioregionalism, supporting grain growers in your area versus long distance transport of chicken feed. This helps close the loop between producer and consumer.
2. Faster weight gains, healthier animals, with fewer disease and illness problems.
3. Higher marketability of chickens, for a better price
4. Reduce the rate of antibacterial resistance that has developed worldwide from the over use of antibiotics in chicken feed.

For those who have larger land holdings and access to equipment, I encourage you to grow some or all of your own grain. You can rotate the chickens through the grain land for extra fertility in alternating years. For an excellent guide to raising, harvesting and feeding small grains, see Gene Logsdon's book *SMALL GRAINS*, published by Rodale Press, Emmaus, Pennsylvania. This book is now out of print but you can get a look at it through your library network.

Water In and Water Out of Your Chicken Tractor System

Chickens lose water through sweat, urine and respiration. In close confinement, the water vapor given off by the chickens can build to unhealthy levels. That's why it's necessary to have a well-ventilated shelter.

Chickens need continual access to fresh, uncontaminated water. Unfortunately, growers who use city tap water for their chickens might be doing the birds a disservice.

There are two chemicals added to many municipal water systems that are unhealthy, both for chickens and for humans. These are chlorine and fluoride.

Chlorine kills bacteria, both good and bad. The chlorine in the tap water kills the beneficial bacteria in the bird's intestinal tract. These bacteria are cells. The lymphocytes (white blood cells) have the task of cleaning the system by consuming the dead cells. This overworks the lymphocytes, taking them away from their primary duty of searching for and consuming cancerous cells in the blood, vascular system, muscle and skin tissue and intestinal tract. As a result, many chickens have greater than normal populations of cancerous cells in their body tissues and fluids.

In humans, byproducts of the use of chlorine can cause cancer, liver and kidney damage, heart and neurological effects and can affect unborn children. Lest you think I'm making all this up, the Environmental Protection Agency has just called for a $50 million dollar, 5-year research program to find out what to do about at least 13,000 public water supplies that are affected. This clean-up will eventually cost America's taxpayers over $1 billion per year, according to the EPA. Not to mention, of course, the billions of dollars in medical bills and the untold suffering of millions of residents who have become ill after long exposure to supposedly safe municipal water.

Fluoride is just as degenerative as chloride, in the same way. It is an insidious, corrosive poison that is a by-product of the aluminum can making industry. According to medical researchers, fluoride is more harmful to the body than the recently banned Alar. Fifty percent of our municipal water systems treat their water with fluoride, even against overwhelmingly strong evidence that it does very little, if anything, to control tooth decay.

In Canada, those communities without fluoride in the drinking water have experienced fewer incidence of tooth decay than those which have treated water. At the same time, those communities with fluoride have a 20% higher rate of cancer. The myth that fluoride fights tooth decay is just that, a myth. That fluoride helps cause cancers in humans, and chickens, is more accurate by far.

Yes, it is true that the average rate of tooth decay has decreased in some areas since the use of fluoride began. I think we can trace this to better programs of teaching dental hygiene in schools. We also now have better toothbrushes and toothpastes, more dental visits, better diet and more flossing. In my opinion, dental hygiene is primarily responsible for the decreased incidence of tooth decay, not fluoride.

There are four ways to overcome the hazards of drinking supposedly safe municipal water.

1. Filter the water first through a sophisticated filtering system.

2. Buy bottled water.

3. Dig a well.

4. Harvest rain water.

Filtering is fairly effective, depending on the capacity and cleansing abilities of the filtering apparatus. It's also fairly expensive, considering the cost of the filtering equipment and installation.

Buying bottled water is expensive. In some areas it costs more than gasoline. Also, there is a chemical reaction taking place between the water and the plastic container, especially when exposed to sunlight. This chemical reaction may result in carcinogens from the plastic being released into the water.

Digging a well is not always practical, possible or cost effective. Drilling the well and installing a pump and water lines can cost thousands of dollars. You still need to test the water to make sure there aren't any contaminants.

So, the best choice, in my opinion, is to harvest rain water from the structure closest to your garden.

Harvesting water is fairly simple and straightforward. The easiest place to look for water to harvest is on your house roof. Just put a gutter on the roof and direct it to a holding tank of some sort. If you have gutters already, just direct the down spout to an area where you can build a holding tank or pond.

The holding tank can be something as simple as a 55-gallon drum, or as elaborate as an above-ground or in-ground swimming pool. If you have room you may want to put in an in-ground pond that can hold all the roof water your house receives. For each 1,000 square feet of roof surface (measured horizontally), you will get 627 gallons of water in each 1-inch rain.

Here in New England the typical house can harvest from 24,000 to 30,000 gallons of rain water per year. A storage facility large enough to handle this volume of water would be huge, compared to what your needs are for chicken watering.

The best scenario, of course, is if you have enough roof surface area to harvest all the water you need into a small pond or holding tank. Concerns are: oxygenation, freezing, utrophication, algae, air and water borne pollutants and diseases, child and pet safety, and aesthetics. Add lime to adjust pH from acid rain. Use a fountain or wind spinner in your pond or holding tank to keep the water agitated. This slows down the algae buildup. Use floating briquettes to keep mosquitoes from breeding, too.

To transport the water to the chicken tractors use a simple wheeled frame similar to a little red wagon. Or, use a garden cart to haul the barrel.

In a larger poultry business you can move barrels of water with a pallet fork mounted on your tractor. The barrel rides on the pallet. Lift the barrel high enough so you can use gravity pressure to clean and fill the waterers at each chicken tractor. Carry the feed in a barrel in the bucket of the tractor so it's a simple one stop operation to feed and water the chickens.

If you want to grow fish for the table or for sale you can make your pond or holding tank large enough to do double duty. In a typical 8 month season here in Vermont we can start with fingerling Tilapia and have harvestable fish to put in the freezer by fall. Weighing 1 to 2 pounds each, they are easy to clean and fillet and make a few good meals each winter. The tilapia will also help keep the water clean and will fertilize it to make it richer for garden irrigation.

Comfrey

Comfrey is a feed supplement you can grow yourself, either in the garden bed or as a hedge planted around the garden. A member of the Borage family, comfrey is rich in vitamins and minerals. Its most important constituent is the chemical allantoin. Allantoin is a primary ingredient in products such as canker medicines, where its ability to aid cell regeneration is important to heal the wound. It is a nitrogenous crystalline substance that appears as white crystals on the dried roots. This substance gives comfrey its remarkable curative, therapeutic and preventive abilities. Allantoin aids cell proliferation and helps immunize against infective diseases, both in humans and livestock.

Protein content of comfrey is highest in the spring, when it can be as much as seven times higher than the protein in soybeans. The following chart lists the major vitamins, nutrients and amino acids contained in comfrey. Naturally, different varieties of comfrey and the differing seasons will affect the available nutrients in the plant, with the spring being highest by some 40%.

Comfrey is a "cut-and-come again" herb that is a recently overlooked and sometimes maligned source of fodder and nutrients for livestock on America's small farms. Herbal teas and tonics and pharmaceutical preparations use most of the comfrey grown commercially in the United States. Over the centuries, comfrey has shown its ability to heal wounds, stop bleeding, treat respiratory ailments, and as a general tonic. Make tea from dried comfrey leaves. Eat young leaves like spinach greens, and use peeled roots in soups.

The plants have a sturdy, upright growth pattern, with leaves shaped like donkey ears. Flowers are creamy-yellow or purple-blue at the top of the 2-foot to 4-foot stalks. Comfrey blooms from April to frost and continues to produce foliage well into the fall season; after most other plants die from frost.

In Europe and England, farmers grow comfrey for human consumption and as a forage crop for livestock. It is a favored herb for poultry, goats, sheep and pigs, with cows being only moderately interested, and horses being only slightly interested in it. Yields can be tremendous, often exceeding 50 tons per acre green weight, with three to four cuttings annually.

One report from Kenya (Dr. Lawrence Hill, *Fertility Without Fertilizers*, 1975), claims 135 tons yield per acre in 12 cuttings. Ecology Action in California grows comfrey as a goat fodder crop and for compost materials. Their yields range from 220 pounds up to 339 pounds per 100 square feet. That is 47 to 72 tons per acre per year.

Comfrey is a very hardy perennial that can withstand temperatures of 40 degrees below zero in a mulched bed. It regenerates itself through root development and seeds. It can become a pernicious weed if allowed to grow uncontrolled in the garden. The best way to eradicate a sprawling comfrey patch is to let pigs root it out, or let the chickens continue to eat the new growth until the plant dies from root exhaustion. Individual plants have a life expectancy of four years, and a well cared for planting can last for 40 years or more.

The plants are heavy feeders, requiring annual replenishment of nitrogen, phosphorous and potassium. They respond very well to liberal applications of fresh chicken or horse manure, and demand plenty of moisture. Straw or leaf mulch is an excellent way to keep the soil around the plants moist while providing slow release nutrients for them. Comfrey responds well to seaweed extract as a foliar spray as well.

Comfrey is difficult to start from seed. Most gardeners start it from root cuttings or plants given to them by gardening friends. Starter plantings are also available from several of the mail order gardening catalogs, (see appendix for listings).

Comfrey prefers a rich soil with a pH range of 6 to 7 and can tolerate full sun or partial shade. It is a good crop for stacking under semi-dense shrubbery and deciduous fruit trees. "Stacking" is the practice of growing several different varieties together that have different levels of top growth and different depths of root growth.

Plant root cuttings or young plants three to six inches deep, two to three feet apart in all directions. If you are using enriched, double dug beds, you can space root cuttings 12 inches apart in a hexagonal pattern. This enables you to plant 159 plants per 100 square feet.

In coming seasons you can increase your comfrey patch by simply digging up the roots, dividing them and replanting. If you allow your comfrey plants to set seed, the seeds will fall near the plant and germinate. Extend your comfrey bed by transplanting these young seedlings.

Within a few weeks after planting, the plants will be large enough for selective harvesting of 3 to 5 inch leaves which you can eat or feed directly to your chickens. If you plan to harvest and dry the comfrey for later use, the first harvest will be ready about 120 days after planting. Cut the entire plant about 2 inches above the crown, hang it in a clean, dry, dark place and leave it to dry slowly. Turn the comfrey frequently and try not to bruise the plants since this will allow molds to enter and spoil your crop. Allowing the comfrey to dry in the sun will be faster, but you will lose much of the nutritional value.

Table 11: Composition of Comfrey

Nutrient	*Percentage*
Protein	21.8 to 33.4
Fat	2.22
Carbohydrates	37.62
Crude fiber	9.38
Ash	15.06
Total digestible nutrients	86.5
Mineral analysis	***Percentage***
Iron	.016
Manganese	.0072
Calcium	1.700
Phosphorus	.820
Vitamins present	***Milligrams per 100 grams***
Thiamine	.5
Riboflavin	1.0
Nicotinic acid	5.0
Pantothenic acid	4.2
Vitamin B12	.07
Vitamin C	100
Vitamin E	30.
Other	
Carotene	.170 parts per million
Allantoin	.18 milligrams per 100 grams
Chlorophyll	
Amino acids:	
tryptophan	
lysine	
isoleucine	
methione	

Comfrey has an aggressive rooting pattern, often drilling down 10 feet or more. The horseradish-like root delivers nutrient rich moisture from deep in the sub-soil to the soil surface. Use comfrey sparingly as a forage or hay due to its high mineral content, high moisture and low fiber content. Your chicken's diet can be 10 to 20 percent comfrey.

In reviewing the above composite chart of comfrey, we can easily see why humans and animals can benefit greatly by its consumption. Comfrey is the fastest known builder of vegetable protein and provides up to seven times the protein found in soybeans. Calcium helps to build strong bones and prevent muscle cramps. Chlorophyll, the life force of all green plants, helps heal diseased tissues and detoxify the blood. Comfrey offers four times as much Vitamin B12 as yeast and is the only plant known to take B12 directly from the soil. Vitamin B12 is important for building healthy blood and will help heal ulcers and arthritis.

Does Comfrey Cause Liver Damage and Central Nervous System Paralysis?

Comfrey has received much attention in recent years because of its constituents *consolidine* and *symphtocynoglossine*. These are two poisonous alkaloids found in the larger leaves (above 5 inches). These have similarities to curare, an arrow poison used by South American Indians. This substance paralyzes the central nervous system.

According to Keats Publishing, New Canaan, Connecticut:

> *The debate and investigation has continued, prompting studies on the alkaloid content and toxicity in three research centers in England. These are reported in an appendix to Lawrence D. Hill's book,* Comfrey: Fodder, Food & Remedy *(Universe Books, 1976) by Dr. D.B.*

Long, who concludes: "The use of comfrey as a food for mankind or animals does not present a toxic hazard from alkaloids, there being no evidence of acute or chronic hepatic reactions either to the direct injection of purified alkaloid or to prolonged consumption of comfrey root flour, which has the highest alkaloid content, by rats."

I'm sure that any astute researcher can find other studies that may point a more accusatory finger at comfrey. I'm mindful, however, that very few things in nature, or from the nation's chemical laboratories, are safe for consumption if taken in extreme doses. Given a choice between using comfrey, or using chemically derived feed supplements in my chicken feed, I choose comfrey.

Countless herbalists and stock breeders around the world are using comfrey daily in their ministrations. It is safe, beneficial, easy to grow, and easy to harvest and store. Your chickens will love it and thrive on it. It aids digestion, which will enhance feed-to-gain ratios and creates less offensive odors in manure. It helps prevent pecking and cannibalism and controls some parasite infestation in the bird's digestion tract. It saves you money on your feed bill and gives you and your customers better tasting meat and eggs.

If possible toxicity of the larger, mature comfrey leaves concerns you, just use them in your compost pile. They are an excellent activator and will return their nutrients to the soil on which you spread your compost.

Kelp
One way to overcome micro-nutrient deficiency in our soil is to use kelp meal. You can use it in meal form as a feed

supplement for livestock, or apply it directly to the land. In its liquid form you can spray it on plant foliage.

I feel that kelp meal is so valuable that I start feeding it as soon as the baby chicks arrive and keep up the ration right through to slaughtering time. Kelp is a complex natural product high in vitamins and minerals. Its most valuable attribute is its richness in trace elements—organic minerals that are both safe and potent.

Lush and otherwise nutritious grass or grains containing adequate amounts of nitrogen, phosphorus and potassium might still fail to supply the nutritional needs of livestock. On poor soil certain trace elements may be missing or not available for plant uptake. Both pasture plants and grazing animals have delicately balanced needs for these trace elements. Too little may produce deficiency symptoms, too much may be poisonous.

One characteristic of kelp as an animal feed, is that the benefits of feeding it to animals seem far out of proportion to the apparent food value of the kelp itself. This is a matter of experience—it results from the observations of farmers and breeders rather than research workers, although more and more research is substantiating users' claims. The fact that kelp modifies the intestinal flora or bacteria of livestock may be the chief cause for the results obtained.

Kelp has been used worldwide for centuries as a rich source of natural organic minerals and vitamins. The ancient Greeks and Chinese used it for medicines, human food and animal feed. Thorvin kelp (*Ascophyllum Nodosum*) contains over 60 elements, 21 amino acids and 13 vitamins, including Vitamin E and Vitamin B12.

When used as a livestock feed additive, kelp increases production and improves performance. It increases appetite and improves digestion. It promotes healthy fur, coats and plumage, and helps to regulate animal heat cycles, increases the number and durability of sperm, improves conception rates, and increases the percentage of normal healthy births. In general, kelp improves the overall health of the animals.

After adding kelp to poultry feed, the grower can expect brighter plumage, increased weight gain and enhanced general alertness. There will be a marked increase in iodine content in eggs. The yolks will be a deeper color, with better pigmentation, improved hatchability, reduction of blood spots, reduced incidence of coccidiosis, less egg breakage and stronger shells. Your poultry will display better feed conversion and improved overall health, with fewer diseases.

Japanese researchers are currently exploring the reduced levels of cholesterol in eggs from chickens who have received kelp supplements in their diet. I can't prove it, but I think the chickens are happier, fight less and have better dispositions, too.

Unfortunately, you can't grow kelp. You will have to buy it from your feed supply store or by mail. One company that sells it as Thorvin Kelp is Necessary Trading Company, One Nature's Way, New Castle, VA 24127, 703-864-5186.

You can see in the charts that kelp contains only tiny amounts of any of the various elements. At first it is hard to understand why such minute amounts of any of these mineral elements can be of any significant benefit to crops or livestock. However, the soil only requires these minerals in tiny—sometimes infinitesimal—amounts.

Table 12: Mineral Analysis of Seaweed (Norwegian *Ascophyllum Nodosum*)

Minerals	**Percentages**	**Minerals**	**Percentages**
Silver	.00004	Sodium	4.180000
Aluminum	.193000	Nickel	.003500
Gold	.000006	Osmium	.000001
Boron	.019400	Phosphorus	.211000
Barium	.001276	Lead	.000014
Calcium	1.904000	Rubidium	.000005
Chlorine	3.680000	Sulfur	1.564200
Cobalt	.001227	Antimony	.000142
Copper	.00635	Silicon	.164200
Fluorine	.032650	Tin	.000006
Iron	.089560	Strontium	.074876
Germanium	.000005	Tellurium	.000001
Mercury	.000190	Titanium	.000012
Iodine	.062400	Thallium	.000293
Potassium	1.280000	Vanadium	.000531
Lantanum	.000019	Tungsten	.000033
Lithium	.000007	Zinc	.0003516
Magnesium	.213000	Zirconium	.000001
Manganese	.123500	Selenium	.000043
Molybdenum	.001592	Uranium	.000004
Other Elements			
Bismuth	Beryllium	Niobium	Cadmium
Chromium	Cesium	Gallium	Indium
Iridium	Palladium	Platinum	Thorium
Radium	Bromine	Cerium	Rhodium
Other Features			
Moisture Content	10.7%	Protein Fat	5.7% 2.6%
Fiber	7.0%	Ash	15.4%

From Norwegian Institute of Seaweed Research

Table 13: Average Analysis of Kelp - Iceland Ascophyllum Nodosum

Macro nutrients	Percent	Minor Nutrients	ppm
Crude Protein	8.6	Cobalt	5
Nitrogen	1.0	Copper	5
Phosphorus	0.1	Iodine	1534
Potassium	8.7	Iron	622
Magnesium	0.7	Manganese	100
Sulfur	2.8	Molybdenum	2
Salt	9.8	Selenium	4
		Zinc	30
Also identified:			
Carbohydrates	alginic acid	mannitol (sugars)	Methylpentosans
laminarin (starch)	fucoidin		
Vitamins:	A B1, B2,	B6 (niacin), B12,	C, D, E, K
Plant Growth Hormones:	auxins	cytokinins	gibberelins

For example, only 2 ounces of Vanadium, a minor nutrient, will be enough to fertilize about 2,000 acres of crops. Lee Fryer, in his book *The New Organic Manifesto*, says, *"That's something like a 'whiff' per acre."*

Seaweed has a chelating ability that makes nutrients more readily available for plant uptake. This enhanced chelation improves cation exchange in garden soil and helps release locked-up minerals.

Kelp also contains growth-producing hormones and can be applied to plant leaves as a foliar spray. The stomata of leaves absorb the growth stimulants gibberellin and auxin, giving better plant growth and development. Seaweed also helps protect plants against light frost, and against certain insect and disease infestations, particularly fusarium in tomatoes and red spider mite in fruit crops.

Kelp Feeding Rate

As a chicken feed supplement, add kelp meal at a rate of 1 to 2 percent of total grain rations. Feed at the higher rate when your stock is under stress, due to travel, disease, weather, reproduction or weaning.

Table 14: Specific Kelp Feeding Rates – Quantity per day

Dairy and Beef Cattle	2 to 4 ounces per day
Heifers and Calves	1 to 2 ounces per day
Horses, Sheep & Goats	1/2 ounce per day
Poultry	1 to 2 percent of feed ration
Large Dogs	1 teaspoon per day
Small Dogs	1/2 teaspoon per day
Cats	1/4 teaspoon per day
Not recommended for rabbits	

The best way to mix Thorvin into the ration is when the feed is being ground and blended, otherwise you can "top dress" it onto already prepared feed. A third method is to mix kelp with salt to feed free choice, cafeteria style. In winter, mix 2 parts kelp to one part salt since the animals eat less salt during the colder months. In summer, reduce the ratio to one part kelp to one part salt. For all range animals, this free choice method may be the most practical. Some farmers choose to mix one part kelp, one part Diatomaceous Earth (see below), and one part salt in their free choice mixture.

Cost of Feeding Kelp as a Feed Supplement

Chickens are, in one measure, poor converters of nutrients. They excrete nearly 80% of the nutritional value of the feed, including the kelp feed supplement. I can't prove it, and the multi-million dollar companies haven't researched it yet, but, I feel that one of the major side benefits of feeding kelp meal is the improved nutrient conversion of the chickens.

We already know that feeding kelp meal causes total feed consumption to go down while health and weight gain improve. It stands to reason that the kelp is enabling the chickens to become better nutrient converters. They are thriving on less feed because they are more effectively utilizing the nutrients contained in the food they do eat.

Each 55 pound bag of Thorvin Kelp costs $49.50, delivered to my farm. That is 90 cents per pound. Each pound of kelp meal will treat 100 pounds of feed, at a cost per pound of .009 cents.

Without the kelp, each chicken will eat 15 pounds of feed to grow to 6 pounds live weight, or 4.25 pounds dressed weight. If I am buying chicken feed at 10 cents per pound, the total cost of feed per chicken will be $1.50.

After adding the kelp to the feed, there is a 10% reduction in feed consumption to achieve the same weight. Total feed consumed then becomes 13.5 pounds per bird. This lowers feed cost to $1.36 per bird.

You save money on the feed bill while getting a healthier, tastier bird, better grazing characteristics and richer, less offensive smelling manure to enrich your soil. Quite a bargain, if you ask me.

Diatomaceous Earth

Diatomaceous Earth (DE) consists of the sedimentary deposits formed from the skeletal remains of a class of algae (*Bacillariophyceae*) that occur in both salt and fresh water and in soil. These remains form diatomite, an almost pure silica, that is ground into an abrasive dust. When the tiny, razor-sharp particles touch an insect, they cause many tiny abrasions, resulting in loss of body water and death by dehydration.

DE is 98% repellent to insects, yet free of dangerous residues. It is digestible by earthworms and harmless to mammals and birds. The dust contains 14 beneficial trace minerals in chelated (readily available) form. Manure and urine carry these minerals into the soil.

Use DE to keep stored feed free of insects. Feed it to poultry and other livestock to control internal parasites. Laying hens will dust themselves in a box of DE to control fleas and lice. It is a digestive activator that helps to control fecal odors, resulting in less offensive smelling manure.

Chapter 8: Diseases and Afflictions

Good Management Will Prevent Most of Them

Over the course of many years of growing chickens, I have experienced only occasional diseases in my home flock. I've talked with other small-scale growers who say this is true for them, as well. By the way, Chicken Pox is a virus spread by direct contact with people who have the disease. It is not transmitted to humans by chickens. The two problems I have had in my broiler flock are curly toe paralysis and breast blister.

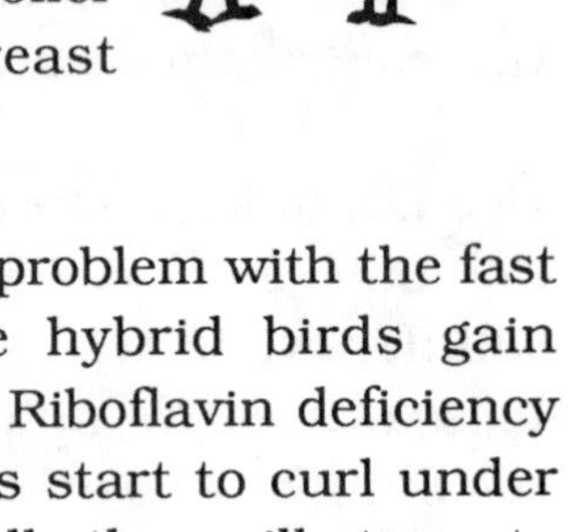

The curly toe paralysis has only been a problem with the fast weight gaining Cornish Cross. These hybrid birds gain weight so fast their legs can't keep up. Riboflavin deficiency can also cause the affliction. Their toes start to curl under and they have trouble walking. Eventually they will starve to death. They just can't get to the feed. In the early stages of curly toe move the chicken to the nurse pen and give it extra yeast for riboflavin. Some times this will cure the affliction.

I think the easiest way to avoid curly toe paralysis is to not buy the breeds that are susceptible to it. A hardier hybrid is the Kosher King, sometimes called the Silver Barred Cross. It is less susceptible to curly toe paralysis than the Cornish Cross. The Kosher King gains weight nearly as well as the Cornish Cross and is a more aggressive forager. This makes the Kosher King more useful in the chicken tractor system. As far as I know, curly toe paralysis is unheard of in the heritage and standard breeds.

The other problem I've had with chickens is breast blister. Like curly toe, breast blister is not prevalent in the heritage and standard breeds. Even though I've raised chickens for years I had never heard of breast blister until I started growing the Cornish Cross hybrids.

Breast blister is a swelling of the skin in the breast area. One grower I talked with feels it happens to his broilers when they crowd under the waterer where it is cooler in the summer. Other growers tell me it happens when the heavy breeds rock on their roosts.

Breast blister, as far as I can tell, is primarily a cosmetic problem on the skin of the breast. It can be trimmed off during processing. It doesn't affect the meat at all and apparently has little effect on weight gain or vigor of the birds.

Coccidiosis is probably the only other chicken ailment that concerns me. A parasite causes this disease. The characteristics of the disease are loose, watery droppings that are sometimes bloody. It usually occurs in young chicks. If I suspect an infection I buy commercial, medicated starter mash for the first two to three weeks, then switch to non-medicated grower pellets. The medicated starter feeds have a coccidiostat that helps prevent the disease.

Antibiotics In Feeds

Medicated feed combats diseases with antibiotics. Unfortunately, the drug passes up the food chain, and can end up in the human body, especially the liver, where the toxins can interfere with our natural immune system. However, I think it is okay to use drugs to keep animals from suffering needlessly or dying. This is particularly true in the case of young chicks. The antibiotics—coccidiostats, for example—will have a chance to move out of the poultry before we eat any of the meat or eggs.

The best preventive, of course, is to raise the chickens as naturally as possible. Give them plenty of good food and clean water, access to sunshine and a place to forage and scratch. Fecal dust is a carrier of disease, too, so clean the waterer and feeder each day when you tend the chickens.

For a really in-depth guide to chicken health there is an excellent new book available by Gail Damerow. Its title is , *The CHICKEN HEALTH Handbook*, (see appendix).

Pecking and Cannibalism

One horrible vice that chickens sometimes develop is pecking each other and in extreme cases, eating each other. The cause of this behavior can be poor nutrition—including lack of enough water or food. Pecking can also be due to over crowding, especially with hens. They need more floor space and nesting privacy.

In my experience with chicken tractors, I have had little trouble with chickens pecking or cannabalizing. The time I had 300 chicks brooding in my garage there was a little pecking on two of the smaller chicks that caused superficial wounds. I separated these two from the larger flock and made sure they got plenty of food, water and quiet. They grew quickly and in a week had recovered and gained enough weight to go back to the brooder without further problems.

Debeaking.

Debeaking is the practice of cutting off slightly more than one-half of the upper beak and blunting the lower beak. This makes it difficult for a bird to grasp feathers or skin. This is industrial agriculture's solution to pecking and cannibalism.

Debeaking is a typically inhumane modern farming practice, and a clear example of fixing the symptom rather than the root problem.

Nippers (like large toenail clippers) are used to manually debeak a bird. Commercial producers use a debeaking machine that has an electrically heated blade that cuts and cauterizes at the same time to stop bleeding. Debeaking can cause damage to the nerves and blood vessels in the circulatory system of the beak. You can imagine how painful this could be, as well as frustrating to the chicken. Birds use their beaks like we use our hands. They use beaks to explore their environment, clean themselves, play, smell, communicate, defend themselves and eat. Mortality from debeaking can be high because the damaged chicks sometimes will not or cannot eat. They will literally starve to death. Most producers debeak at about one week old; some do it as early as one day old. In my opinion, debeaking is among the cruelest things you can do to a bird both physically and psychologically.

Figure 16: Debeaking

I don't recommend you debeak chickens in your chicken tractors. They need their beaks to forage for seeds, bugs and weeds. Poultry foraging in your garden is part of the key to the chicken tractor system. The chances of you having pecking problems will be minimal if you provide good nutrition and do not crowd your flock into too small an area.

Chapter 9: Predators

I've grown chickens in several areas of the country; such as the river bottoms of southwestern Missouri and northeastern Oklahoma, the sand dunes of Cape Cod, and the broad lake valleys of Vermont. There are several varmints common to all these areas: raccoons, coyotes, feral cats, bob cats, red and gray foxes, minks, weasels, big snakes (not in Vermont) and worst of all, the neighbor's dogs.

In a typical hen yard or on free range, without the protection of the chicken tractor, losses to predators can be quite high. Just the other day I heard from a poultry grower in Missouri who has lost 200 free-range hens to foxes in the past year.

In my experience, moving the chicken tractors daily seems to make predators suspicious, so they don't bother the chickens. Having said that, however, I need to point out that varmints of all kinds will be eager to take a crack at your homegrown poultry.

Rats & Mice

Rats and mice are common inhabitants of farms and fields. They love poultry feed and will chew holes in feed bags if they have access to them. Rats will also kill baby chicks and drag them into their burrows.

These rodents love hiding places they find in conventional chicken houses. Spaces between walls, under floors and around junk make great rodent hotels. Luckily, with your portable chicken tractors, there are few places for a mouse or rat to set up housekeeping. The chicken tractor doesn't have walls or floors where the critters can hide and build nests.

I keep grain stored in galvanized garbage cans with the lid secured with a bungee cord. This makes the feed for my small flock rodent proof—even raccoon proof, and I have yet to see any rat using the bungee cords to jump off the trash can for a cheap thrill.

Domestic Cats and Dogs

Since I've been using chicken tractors my only problem with predators has been a neighborhood dog trying to dig under the pen when I use it in a deep mulch system. I stopped that by laying chicken wire alongside the pen on all four sides and pegging it to the ground with pins made from bent coat hangers.

My neighbor's dog sometimes runs and jumps and barks in front of the chicken tractor, scaring the dickens out of the birds. One way to prevent this, short of tying up your neighbor's dog, is to run a hog wire fence or electric fence around the perimeter of the pens, at least ten feet out. The biggest danger from dogs is their barking and chasing, causing the chickens to crowd in a corner where they pile up and suffocate, or die of fright.

The best way to prevent dogs and cats from bothering your chickens is to teach them how to behave around chickens. Barking and chasing is simply not acceptable and we reprimand accordingly. Even my cats have learned to leave our baby chickens alone—although they will sit and observe the chicks for hours. All my pets know what no! means and know what is acceptable behavior.

Foxes, Coyotes, Raccoons, Weasels & Other Critters.

Several years ago—before I started using chicken tractors—raccoons pulled the chicken wire off my hen house window to get at the birds. That window was 6-feet off the ground. I think the raccoons climbed a nearby tree, dropped down on the roof, and reached over the roof edge to pry the window open.

If you live in an area where chicken loving critters present a greater than normal problem, you can provide extra protection for the chicken tractor. Install a portable electric fence around the garden area. The new net-style electric sheep fence is especially effective. Bait the fence with peanut butter so the wildlife will try to lick it off. This guarantees they will get a healthy shock to their tongue that will convince them that these electric fences mean business.

Don't tempt fate and a hungry canine. If you know coyotes or foxes are living in your wood lot, don't put your chicken pens out there without some kind of extra protection.

Another way to protect the chickens, if you do need to put them near the woods, is to install a dog run parallel to the field edge and leash your dog to it each evening.

A fox will often kill several birds and sometimes leaves them partially buried. Raccoons, for all their fastidiousness, can be gruesome diners. If chickens are sleeping too close to the pen sides, the raccoon can reach its paw and powerful claws through the wire to grab a chicken and will literally pull it apart alive. If a raccoon gets in with the chickens it will usually eat the crops (throats) of chickens and will decapitate some of the birds. A raccoon will return every few days for another dinner if he gets the chance.

Minks and weasels tend to kill several birds at irregular intervals. Their trademarks are small bites around the head and neck.

Figure 17: Ways to Predator Proof Your Chicken Tractor

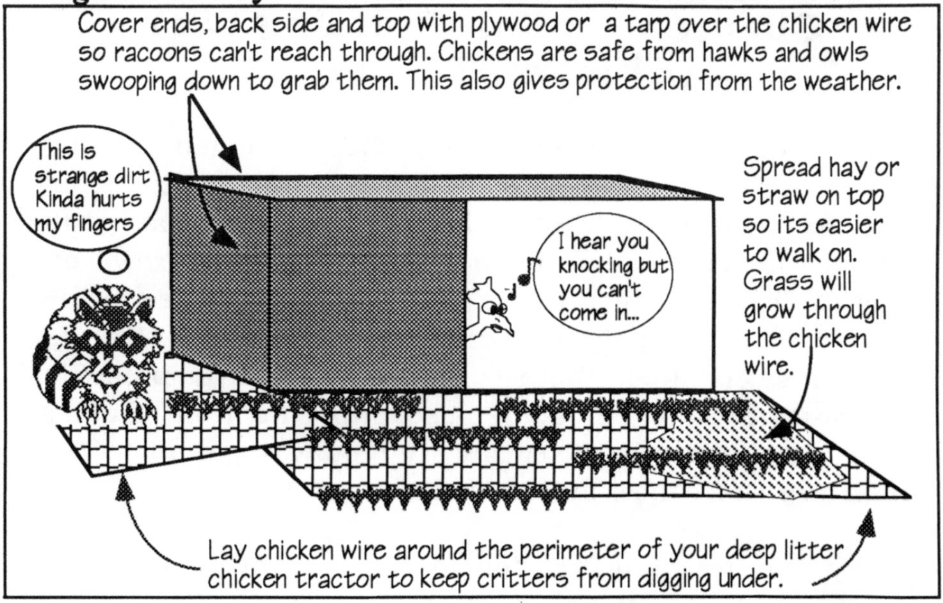

Predatory Birds.

Owls and hawks love chicken dinners. They tend to kill one or two birds, usually at night. They leave behind the carcass except for the head and neck. I have yet to lose any poultry to predatory birds, primarily because the chickens are always inside the chicken tractor with its protective lid. Keep in mind that owls and hawks mainly eat mice, moles and other potential pests. They help keep nature in balance.

The ultimate solution to the varmint problem, of course, is to shoot or trap them all. To me this isn't an acceptable option. I enjoy the occasional siting of the wildlife far too much to ever want to eradicate them from my land. Many of the varmints, too, are predators of mice, moles and other grain eating herbivores that can cause problems in the grain fields if their populations get out of hand. It is far better we coexist with the predators and let them help us keep a healthy balance of natural life in our meadows, fields and forests.

Chapter 10: Soil Building With Chicken Tractors

Today's chemically intensive and tillage oriented farming practices have resulted in soils deficient in trace elements and micro nutrients. These deficiencies become apparent in the nutritional content of the grasses and grain grown on these soils. Consequently, we are seeing deficiencies in the health of the animals maintained on these crops. It goes without saying, then, that we humans who eat the products of these infertile fields are also suffering from dietary deficiencies. These deficiencies are readily apparent in our nation's rising cancer and heart disease statistics.

Many soil nutrient deficiencies can be overcome with applications of compost and livestock manure. Throughout our American history we've had plenty of positive experiences using livestock in crop rotations to renew the earth with manure. Thomas Jefferson, in 1793, wrote of *"a moveable airy cow house, to be set up in the middle of the field which is to be dunged, and soil our cattle in that thro' the summer as well as winter, keeping them constantly up & well littered."*

If we knew that much 200 years ago, why did we forget? Somewhere in our nation's history we lost sight of what James Madison, our fourth president, said in 1818, *"Nothing is more certain than that the continual cropping without manure deprives the soil of its fertility. It is equally certain that fertility may be preserved or restored by giving to the earth animal or vegetable manure equivalent to the matter taken from it."*

In today's agriculture, we have a situation that is the exact opposite of what Jefferson and Madison both recommended. With the on-set of monocrop farming in the last four decades, we have seen livestock disappear from thousands and thousands of acres of farmland, to be replaced by year after year of cash grain crops. Monocropping results in soil erosion from wind and rain. The soil lies bare and unprotected by vegetation for most of the year. Without livestock manure there is not a good way to replenish fertility and organic matter. The structure and tilth of the soil degenerates year by year.

Soil loss from these grain fields is enormous. Some reports indicate that growers lose as much as 4 bushels of topsoil for each bushel of grain produced. Nationally, topsoil losses average 4 tons per acre per year, which is 10 times greater than average natural soil formation. In mid-western grain fields it is not uncommon to experience topsoil losses of as much as 11 tons per acre per year!

One hundred years ago, topsoil in some areas of the Great Plains measured nearly a dozen feet deep. Today, we measure remaining topsoil in inches. In some areas less than 4-inches remains, and in extreme cases the land has become desert.

I've spent years watching the land after heavy rains. To see the good brown earth continually being washed off the fields into nearby lakes and streams is alarming. This is the condition that writer and farmer Edward Faulkner described as "*watching the farmer's fortune wash downstream*".

I think the first thing we need to do as a nation is to stop growing cash grains on fields that are subject to erosion and flooding. We should return these marginal fields to pasture, vegetated wetlands and forest land. Then, concentrate our crop producing energies on the remaining good land.

We need to restore our fields to their past levels of high organic matter and fertility. Then, we need to use rotational grazing of poultry and other livestock, combined with green manure cover crops and sensible crop rotations, to increase yields. Increased yields from properly enriched fields will more than make up for taking our marginal acres out of production.

I feel there will be many immediate and positive results from this movement away from plowing and planting every last acre of land that is available to us, regardless of its suitability for farming. Our air will be cleaner because there will be less dust in it. The streams, rivers, lakes and oceans will be cleaner because of reduced erosion and silting.

Our use of fossil fuels for farming will decrease since we will be concentrating our food growing energies on smaller pieces of real estate. Our livestock health—and human health—will improve, as food animals return to a grass based diet that is easier for them to digest and helps them produce meat that is lower in fat and cholesterol.

Some farmers are being pushed onto marginal land because much of our good land is being lost to increased residential, commercial and industrial development. This results directly from our steadily increasing population. In my lifetime our world population has doubled. My remaining life expectancy of 30 years will see another doubling of our population. So, in my lifetime there will have been a quadrupling of the world population.

In the next thirty years the demands for land for housing, institutional, commercial and industrial development will be enormous. As prices skyrocket for buildable land the areas available for farming will become smaller and smaller. This process is already exceedingly acute where we need farm land most, at the fringes of our towns and cities.

Nearly 1/3 of our nation's farmland, 320 million acres, lies at the urban edge. On this land, we raise 86% of all fruits and vegetables, 80% of all dairies and 45% of our meat, poultry and fish. This land is under intense pressure from development, pollution and erosion. Each day we lose nearly 17,000 acres of tillable land, or 60 million acres per decade.

In the past year alone we lost nearly 2.5 million acres to development, and several times that much to erosion, salinization, pollution and loss of soil fertility. It doesn't take a rocket scientist to figure out that if these losses continue unabated we are at risk of creating huge famine within the very near future.

It seems like a farfetched idea, I know, to think we will ever have famine or new deserts forming in America. It wasn't too many years ago, though, that the droughts that caused the Dust Bowl did just that, giving us a dire warning of even more deserts to come. If you doubt this is true, look across the ocean to countries like Sudan and Ethiopia to see what the final harvest of over-population, over-farming and over-development might be.

Both of these countries, as late as 1940, were 40% forested and had more than adequate food supplies for their people. Now they are both nearly 100 percent desert, and the population rests in the grip of a terrible famine that appears to be unsolvable.

Twice As Much Food on Half As Much Land

In the next 30 years it is entirely possible that our farm land will decrease by half, while our expanding population's food demand will double. Our nation will then have the necessity of growing twice as much food on half the land. Can we do it? I think so.

Allan Savory, developer of Holistic Resource Management, in Albequerque, New Mexico, says, *"It's becoming increasingly clear that we will all soon be managing land of smaller units of greater complexity."*In an earlier chapter I described the work of Steve Rioch at Ohio University and the work of John Jeavons at Ecology Action in California. They have been able to prove, beyond any shadow of doubt, that they can improve vegetable yields by 4 to 31 times the current national average. Even grain yields will double or triple with intensive growing techniques.

Now, these increases are possible to all of us, if we take the time to study successful, intensive growing methods and replicate them in our own gardens and fields. The important distinction between John and Steve and me is that they are growing a vegetarian diet, while I still, at least for the near future, prefer to eat meat.

It may be a far gone conclusion that at some point in our nation's future we will all become vegetarian. I believe this will happen because the declining land base will make meat so expensive that many of us won't be able to afford it. This is already true in Japan, where steak sells for as much as $24 per pound.

The apparent answer to an increased population and declining farm land is for all of us to become vegetarian. We and our next generation will eat food grown on land currently being used to raise livestock feed. However, most of the U.S. population is still eating a meat-based diet, and most of them are unwilling to give it up. Currently here in America, less than 5 percent of our population is vegetarian.

Some 40% of that group eats some meat occasionally, primarily fish and poultry.

It seems unlikely that the remaining 95 percent of our population who are meat eaters are going to change their diet overnight. So, it's not likely that our national meat-based diet will change significantly soon. Rather it will erode gradually as more and more people find our current diet is too expensive, not only in dollars and cents but in health and environmental costs as well.

How Can Chicken Tractors Help?

The answer, at least for the near future, is to adjust our farming methods to more pasture and less grain. This means more intensive livestock management on the pastures, and less reliance on confinement feeding of livestock such as in feedlots.

In the poultry industry today we have only a few companies, each growing millions of broilers each year. Let's think instead about having thousands of small-scale growers, each producing only thousands of birds each year, and doing it on pasture with supplemental grain.

Three important benefits—along with many lesser benefits—will result from such a paradigm shift. First, consumers will have access to good tasting, healthy chickens. Second, many new farmers will be able to make all or part of their living on their land. Third, and perhaps most important, there will be a significant reversal of deterioration in our nation's farms, health and environment.

The chicken tractor system is nothing more than management intensive, high density, short duration rotational grazing. I think it's important to point out here that the chicken tractor method can apply just as well to all manner of livestock. Dairy cows, beef, horses, sheep, pigs, and goats can all be grown successfully using high density, short duration rotational grazing.

Time after time it's been proven that rotational grazing can improve the land, produce a superior product, and make more money for the farmer than confinement feeding. Regardless of which livestock are in the system. We cannot deny these facts, although our national policy makers can ignore them.

Sensible and humane livestock production has to become part of our nation's cultural ethic. Consider recycling, as an example. Five years ago none of us knew how to, now we're all doing it as a day to day routine. If the Congress of the United States will get behind this rotational grazing idea and mandate an end to grain based confinement feeding, we will see an immediate, incredible national shift to a healthier diet, a healthier environment and a healthier nation.

In the meantime, until that glorious day arrives, we can only continue our experiments and demonstrations. Our efforts will have an effect on our neighbors and friends, and there will be a swelling pool of knowledge. Eventually the nation's population will see the benefits of rotational grazing and will force our government to take it seriously.

So, as poultry growers, either for our own use or for sale, we need to start improving our land and our incomes with chicken tractors. Use the chicken tractors to fertilize your gardens or farm fields, so that you can grow more of your own food, and enough to sell to earn either a full-time or part-time income from your land.

How Does Soil Fertility Happen?
Soil forms by the decomposition of organic matter—materials that were once living—into humus. The decomposition takes place when the decomposer organisms--earthworms, bacteria, fungi, etc.—eat the organic matter.

It's an interesting notion, but soil doesn't deepen, it uppens. As each year's growth dies and falls to the earth, it decays and turns into humus. This humus contains the nutrients, vitamins and minerals that the next year's plant growth requires. It is an ongoing cycle, with the soil dwellers providing the nutrients for the plants, and the plants growing the biomass to feed the soil dwellers. For centuries humans have searched for the perpetual motion machine. All along they've had it, right at their very feet, in the ground we walk on.

Anything that was once living can become soil organic matter and then humus. That's why, when we mulch the soil it will eventually become richer as the mulch decays and turns into humus—top soil.

We can destroy this valuable layer of top soil—humus and organic matter—in one of several ways. We can plow and till the soil until it becomes finely granulated, subject to wind and water erosion. We can plant continuous crops in the soil, remove all the biomass as feed for distant livestock and humans, and not allow any organic materials back to the earth to feed the soil dwellers.

Another way we can destroy soil is to use astringent fertilizers that over-stimulate soil dwellers, causing a rapid depletion of the organic matter. We can also use toxic chemicals that kill the soil dwellers, thereby totally disabling the cycle in which plants provide food for the soil life and the soil life provides food for the plants.

The chicken tractor system interrupts all of these methods of soil destruction, replacing them with a system that very closely resembles the natural processes. As the chickens eat the greenery inside their pen they remove the need for herbicides. The manure from the chickens replaces the need for synthetic fertilizers. The organic material in the chicken manure—about 40 percent of the volume—feeds the soil life, which in turn feeds the plant life that feeds the chicken. All of this in nature's symbiotic harmony.

The trick, of course, is to manage the chicken tractor rotations in a way best suited to providing the needs of the soil, the chickens, and the farmer. This means that we don't want to leave the chickens in one place too long, lest they deposit more manure than the soil can immediately handle. That could lead to toxicity and perhaps even run-off or nitrate leaching.

If it is necessary to leave the chicken tractor in the same place for a prolonged period, then add carbon material such as straw or dry hay. This carbonaceous material acts as a buffer, a primitive bio-filter, to dilute the effects of the nitrogen rich chicken manure.

How Much Organic Matter Do We Need in the Soil?

I've always thought of organic matter as being the heart of the soil. It provides food for the soil dwellers, who in turn make the nutrients available to the plants. Organic matter acts as a buffer against wind and water erosion. A soil that is only 1 percent organic matter will be continually at risk of blowing or washing away unless it is continually covered with plant life. A soil that has 5 percent organic matter will have a crumb structure suitable for withstanding wind and water erosion.

A rich soil having a 5 percent level of organic matter absorbs many times more rain water before eroding and will retain water much longer. Plants growing in a soil with sufficient organic matter will be far less stressed by lack of water between rain falls. The organic matter acts like a living sponge. It is a giant reservoir that holds the water and releases it slowly for plant use.

Organic matter starts the process whereby the soil becomes more fertile, enabling the grower to achieve increased yields from crops. In one test I did several years ago I found that tomato plants in soil containing less than 1 percent organic matter would yield about 2 pounds of fruits per plant. In the adjacent plot—where soil organic matter stood at 5 percent—the tomato plants yielded from 7 to 20 pounds per plant.

Each type of soil has an optimum and a maximum yield potential. To maximize yields it is usually necessary to add extra fertilizer, particularly nitrogen, to the soil. This added nitrogen often has an unwanted side effect of causing excessively rapid decomposition of the soil organic matter. I think it's better to strive for optimal production yields. Ask the soil to produce yields that are sustainable without costly and degenerative applications of nitrogen.

To achieve optimal production yields—versus maximum—requires us to replenish the soil organic matter on a regular basis, either annually or bi-annually, depending on the crop we are growing. The fastest and most complete way to add organic matter to the soil is with applications of well-balanced compost. Other ways to achieve increases in soil organic matter are through cover cropping green manures and with sheet mulching. Neither of these are as immediately effective as compost.

Using Compost to Increase Organic Matter in the Soil. Depending on soil type and parent material there are about 2,000,000 pounds of soil per acre foot. When you have a soil test done, be sure to ask the laboratory to test for the percentage of organic matter in your soil. Anywhere from less than 1 percent to more than 40 percent of the top layer of the soil is organic matter. The dry, sandy soil of the arid west is often lower than 1 percent organic matter. The muck soils of southern Canada may have as much as 40 percent organic matter. Most soils in the United States are somewhere between 1 percent and 5 percent.

Adding 20 tons per acre of compost to the soil will increase the organic matter by about 1 percent. Each pound of compost will contain about 1/2 pound of organic matter, with the rest being made up of water and air. This 1 percent gain in soil organic matter will require about 1 pound of compost per square foot of land.

Compost weighs about 1,000 to 1,100 pounds per cubic yard, depending on the moisture content and the origin of the raw materials. Therefore, you will need about 40 cubic yards of good compost per acre. In your garden beds this amounts to about 3 cubic feet of compost per 100 square feet. That's about a 1-inch layer.

In soil reclamation you will want to apply this amount of compost each year until the soil organic matter measures above 5 percent. Then you can decrease compost applications to every other year or every third year. This will enable you to expect optimal yields on a sustained basis.

Making good compost requires that you have the right combination of air, water, carbon materials and nitrogen materials. Introduce air to the compost pile by turning it or with venting pipes or layering in materials such as cornstalks that will naturally convect air through the pile.

Water can come from natural rain fall. During dry periods you may want to add water to the pile. The compost pile needs to be damp, like a wrung out sponge. If it is too dry or too wet the decomposers—bacteria, fungi, earthworms—can't do their job.

The proper carbon to nitrogen ratio in the compost pile is about 30:1. As an example, add one-part leaves (C/N 50:1) to one-part green grass clippings (C/N 10:1). The resulting C/N is 30:1. You arrive at this number by adding the materials together, i.e., 50:1 plus 10:1 = 60:1 divided by 2 = 30:1. Well-balanced compost--made from proper combinations of carbon and nitrogen materials—will have an N-P-K ratio of about 1-1-1. This means each of the macronutrients—nitrogen, phosphorous and potassium—is about 1 percent of the total volume. The following chart shows the carbon to nitrogen ratio of a few common materials:

Under most circumstances the decomposition process in the compost pile will reduce the volume of materials by about 50 percent. In other words, if you put in 10 tons of raw materials you'll get back about 5 tons of compost.

If we add 20 tons per acre of compost to the soil, and the compost contains 1 percent nitrogen (N), we are adding 400 pounds of N per acre. Is that too much? No. The nitrogen binds to the organic matter of the compost, where it remains available for slow release. Only about 50 percent of the nitrogen value of the organic matter will release during the first year. In the following year another 50 percent will release, and so forth, until the nitrogen store is depleted.

Table 15: Ratio of Carbon to Nitrogen in Common Materials

Carbon Materials:	**Carbon to Nitrogen Ratio:**
Leaves	50:1
Straw	80:1
Dry hay	50:1
Sawdust	300-500:1
Nitrogen Materials:	
Green grass clippings	10:1
Food waste	10:1
Livestock manure	10:1
Slaughter waste	10:1

The organic matter will hold the organic N until the plants need it. Inorganic N, on the other hand, is immediately available for plant use. The inorganic N that isn't used quickly by the plants will be susceptible to leaching.

Chickens Add Fertilizer and Organic Matter to the Soil

If you use the chicken tractor system to raise chickens in your garden you can expect soil fertility and organic matter content to increase in your garden beds practically overnight. This happens because the chicken is not able to convert all of its feed to either meat or eggs. Chickens excrete an average of 75% nitrogen, 80% phosphorous and 85% potassium that is in the animal feed.

A mature hen will eat about 80 to 90 pounds of feed per year, and produce about 50 pounds of nutrient rich manure. A broiler will eat about 15 pounds of feed and will excrete about 10 pounds of manure over a 8 week period. About 40 percent of this manure is organic matter.

Therefore, if you raise 10 hens in a 40 square foot pen, and move the pen daily, the hens will be depositing about 500 pounds of manure per year on your garden beds. You can rotate these 10 hens from bed to bed in a 30 day cycle. That means they will spend one day on each site and not return to that site for 30 days.

This rotational system will cover 1,200 square feet, about the size of a 30-foot by 40-foot family garden. Thanks to the nutrients and organic matter in the chicken manure you will have fertile beds next year in which to grow your garden.

Use the deep mulch system if you don't have enough garden space to move your chickens each day. The advantage of adding mulch to the chicken tractor daily is that it will interrupt the loss of nutrients to volatilization. If you don't protect the chicken manure on the soil surface, anywhere from 30 to 90 percent of the nitrogen can be lost. Nearly 50 percent of that loss will occur in the first 24 hours. The longer the nitrogen lays exposed the greater the percentage of loss.

Another advantage to the dry hay or straw mulch is to buffer the impact of the nitrogen in the chicken manure. The carbon nature of the mulch will help lock up the nitrogen, releasing it slowly so that the following crop plants don't get an oversupply of nitrogen. Too much nitrogen in the soil can lead to excessive foliage growth in the plants. This may actually retard the yields of the plant. The carbon material helps to buffer any potential nitrogen overload.

Using Rotational Pens to Build Soil Fertility.

Using poultry in a rotational grazing sequence is a good way to add fertility to your garden quickly. Each day move the portable shelter-pen to a new spot, leaving behind a residue of manure and organic matter.

As soon as I move my portable pen I broadcast cover crop seed, either buckwheat or winter rye, on the old site. Then I use a garden hoe to loosen the soil, about one inch deep, to cover the seeds I've just sown. Then I apply a light layer of compost, shredded leaves, dry hay or loose straw. This simple, quick technique mixes the newly deposited layer of chicken manure into the soil surface and covers the new seeds to ensure good germination.

By the time the cover crop has germinated and grown to 4-6 inches height the next batch of chickens is ready to graze this spot. Over the course of the season each spot gets visited by the chickens three times. After the first and second visits I use cover crops. After the third visit I just cover the site with a light coat of mulch to protect it over winter. Next spring this site will be easy to prepare as a garden bed.

This activity incorporates the nutrient-rich chicken manure into the soil quickly so those valuable vitamins and gases don't escape. Covering the seeds with compost or shredded leaves protects them from birds. The cover holds the moisture in the soil and helps provide the seed-to-soil contact that is so critically important to good seed germination. The root mass left from the previous crop stays in the soil to decay. As the roots decompose they leave channels that feed and house soil life and enhance drainage and moisture capillarity.

Why Not Rotary Till?
I don't rotary till the site before planting. The only reason we ever need to use mechanical tillage in the soil is to break up hardpan or to prepare a seed bed. The very act of tilling itself, if done too often or not done properly, builds hardpan

and destroys soil tilth. Pulverized clay and silt particles created during tillage leach in heavy rainfall. Gravity and hydraulic pressure pull the pulverized particles to the underlying firm sub-soil where they stratify and compact, forming hardpan.

Hardpan is easy to create, hard to cure and totally disabling to garden crops. It interferes with earthworm migration from surface to sub-soil. It blocks root growth, holds heavy rainfall near the surface, and blocks the capillary action that brings water from the sub-surface water table to the surface when the plants need it during dry spells.

Tillage implements mix good soil (the surface loam), with poor soil (the sub-surface sand and gravel). This creates only fair soil, or worse. Too much oxygen pumped into the soil causes oxidation and poor capillarity. It over-stimulates soil bacteria and disallows seed-to-soil contact for optimal seed germination.

If the area you are working is too large to work up a seed bed efficiently with a hand hoe, you can still use the rotary tiller. Just run the tiller at a low idle rather than full power. This gives the tines a slow speed. Set the tine depth as shallow as possible while incorporating the top mulch and the cover crop seeds. With a slow rotary speed you will be less apt to pulverize the soil, and with the shallow depth you will not be interfering as much with the soil structure or moving the sub-soil towards the surface and vice versa.

The roots and top growth of the cover crop that follows the chickens act as a biomass trap. This holds the nitrogen and other macro and micro nutrients in the roots and top growth. The nutrients contained in the biomass return to the chickens in their next grazing rotation. If you till under the cover crop, the nutrients return to the soil. If you mow the top growth to harvest the biomass for green manure you can use it in the compost. I don't have to buy any fertilizer for my garden crops. They get plenty from the residual poultry manure and green matter, and from compost applications.

Sheet Mulching to Aid Soil Fertility.

There are some disadvantages to planting a cover crop after each pen move. Planting the cover crop takes time, labor, equipment and seeds. In most cases the ground under the chicken tractor is damp enough for seed germination but you will have to irrigate during the dry seasons. At least until the cover crop has germinated and is strong enough to send its roots in search of water below the surface.

With this cover crop scheme the bare soil lies unprotected until the seeds germinate and grow tall enough to provide damage control. This can take two to three weeks during which time your soil is at risk of eroding from wind or heavy rain fall.

The alternative to growing cover crops is to use sheet mulch. After moving the pen, simply scatter straw or dry hay on the site and leave it. The nitrogen and other nutrients in the layer of chicken manure will enable the decomposer bacteria to turn the layer of mulch into compost and eventually into humus.

While this decomposition is going on, the surface mulch gives several other benefits. It protects the soil and soil dwellers from harsh sunlight, and prevents wind blown or rain water erosion. The happy reward is richer soil with less work.

When you are rotating your chicken tractor over a 30 day period you just add another layer of mulch to the beds on the second and third rotation through the garden.

You can even use this method in larger farms. There is an attachment for unrolling large round bales that fits on the 3-point hitch of the farm tractor. Just drive along the beds unrolling the bales wherever you need them. Through the fall, winter and early spring the hay will decompose while it is acting as protector of the soil and keeping the nutrients from escaping or leaching. Don't put the mulch on too thick because it is difficult to till under when preparing a seed bed. About 1 to 3 inches is enough, I think.

The mulch causes cooler soil that will delay soil preparation in the spring by a few days, but that's not such a problem. It's usually better to wait a few days, until the air and soil temperatures are at the proper levels, before planting spring crops.

The later planted crops will germinate and grow better, faster and probably will mature at about the same time, or within a few days of the early crops. By delaying plantings until the soil warms up you will often avoid cold snaps that occur late in the spring. Crops planted too early are often lost during a hard frost.

This mulching system can save money on fertilizer, tilling, and compost making. This system works best in permanent beds, and is ideal for the home grower or small-scale market grower.

Wild and Wonderful Earthworms.

One component of the successful mulching system is the reliance on earthworms to do a major portion of the decomposition of the sheet mulch. To encourage earthworms to take an active role in your garden program you need to make sure the soil pH is near neutral.

Earthworms work best in a soil that has a plentiful supply of calcium. You can add calcium to your soil by adding lime. The earthworms use the calcium to make pellets for use in their digestion process. Acid soils interfere with their ability to get calcium. More earthworms will inhabit neutral or nearly neutral soils than they will in acid soil.

Earthworm castings are 5 to 11 times richer in plant nutritional value than the raw materials the earthworms are eating. The increase has to do with the secretions in the worm's digestive tract and calciferous glands.

To encourage earthworm proliferation in your soil reduce tillage and add organic matter. Tests at the National Soil Tilth Lab in Ames, Ohio, show that a soil with a high population of earthworms can absorb a 2-inch rain in 12 minutes. While a soil without earthworms will take 12 hours to absorb a 2-inch rain.

Nitrogen Needs of Various Vegetables.
A big advantage to using the chicken tractor system is that you don't have to buy fertilizers or compost in subsequent years. This can save you a great deal of money. Perhaps you will want to buy greensand, rock dust and other amendments, but not fertilizer. You can save up to $300 to $500 per acre in fertilizer and as much as $1,500 per acre in compost.

Trying to determine how much nitrogen to apply per year in your garden beds is difficult, to say the least. The biggest problem you'll have is in trying to figure out how much nitrogen you already have in the soil. Because nitrogen is so mobile, most soil tests don't give an accurate reading. Also, you don't know how much nitrogen it will take to feed the soil life as well as the plants you hope to grow in the soil.

There are some general figures that give you a target to strive for. These figures are for soils that are low in fertility. I use them here primarily as a reference to check the general soil health. This is not a rigid recommendation of exactly what you need in your soil for good crops.

Any nitrogen already in the soil needs to stay in place to feed the soil microbes. Add the amount of nitrogen you need to grow your intended crop without depleting the soil's store of nitrogen.

Table 16: Nitrogen Needs of Common Vegetables

Vegetable	**Nitrogen (lb/acre)**
Beans	50
Broccoli	100
Cucumbers	100
Lettuce	90
Onions	75
Peas	75
Potatoes	180
Sweet Corn	110
Tomatoes	100
Winter Squash	75

This table gives the amount of nitrogen fertilizer your crops will need during the growing season. The allowances are for a first year garden that has poor soil. These figures do not account for any nitrogen already in the soil. They also do not reflect the amount of nitrogen in the compost or sheet mulch you are applying to the garden.

Most, if not all, the nitrogen requirement for these plants is in the chicken manure being made available from your chicken tractor rotations. In the case of low nitrogen feeders such as beans, onions and peas you might want to leave the chicken tractor on that bed for less time, perhaps only 1/2 day. In the case of high nitrogen feeders such as sweet corn and potatoes you can leave the chickens on those beds longer to accumulate more manure, perhaps two full days.

As they get older the chickens will deposit more manure. You can move the younger chickens less frequently, and the older chickens more often to adjust the amount of fertilizer per bed.

Seaweed Meal and Seaweed Extract

The key to improved crop yields, both in plants and in livestock, is in building the best soil possible using materials that are at hand. In some cases, especially in new gardens or in reclaiming worn out land, the soil is just not healthy and fertile enough to provide the macro and micro nutrients demanded by the plants.

In this case, fertility and plant health can be improved, sometimes dramatically, by using foliar sprays containing seaweed extract and fish emulsion. It is available in products such as Foliogro and Seamix.

Seaweed meal supplement in chicken feed is one of the surest ways to start building balanced fertility in the soil. If seaweed meal has not had time to cycle through your garden through the chicken tractor, then consider spraying your crops with liquid seaweed extract.

Seaweed contains growth hormones including auxins, gibberellins, and cytokinins. All of these are chemical messengers produced naturally in minute quantities by the plant. Cytokinins are particularly important, since they increase the speed of cell division and aid the plant in the process of photosynthesis.

In their book, *The Soul of Soil*, Grace Gershuney and Joseph Smillie, write *"Foliar supplementation may also be necessary as an annual practice in some soil and climate situations. In cold northern soils, foliar fertilizers may be necessary each spring to supply nitrogen and phosphorus. In alkaline and high organic matter (peat and muck) soils, micro nutrient sprays like iron may be necessary since certain minerals may never be available under these conditions."*

"Some minerals (such as calcium and boron) are easily absorbed but poorly translocated, while others (such as iron and copper), move easily through the vascular system but don't readily cross the leaf epidermis (to gain access to the stomata). Temperature, light, oxygen, pH and energy availability all affect leaf absorption but the most important is leaf surface moisture."

Foliar sprays work best when applied early in the morning, especially on a cloudy day. Adding a drop of surfactant to the spray mix can help deionize the leaf surface and aid the stomata in absorbing the nutrients. Stomata are tiny, mouth-like openings on the leaf surface that enable the plant to exchange gaseous aerosols and mists with the surrounding atmosphere. Spraying should also coincide with the stage of plant growth when nutrients are in high demand by the plant but root intake is low.

Leaves--and their tiny stomata--cannot accept large amounts of macro nutrients such as nitrogen, phosphorus and potash. They can, however, accept valuable, minute quantities of micro nutrients and trace elements, particularly the growth stimulators auxin, gibberellins and cytokinins.

There is a complex and not totally understood interrelationship between these stomata and the ambient surroundings of the plant. Authors Christopher Bird and Peter Tompkins, in their book *Secrets of the Soil*, (see appendix) report on the unusual results achieved by Dan Carlson, originator of *Sonic Bloom*. He recorded pre dawn bird sounds and played them back to crops to stimulate the leaf stomata to open wide for receiving nutrients from foliar spray.

Playing this sound back to the plants *"induced stomata to imbibe more than seven times the amount of foliar-fed nutrients, and even absorb invisible water vapor in the atmosphere that exists, unseen and unfelt, in the driest of climatic conditions."*

Minneapolis music teacher, Michael Holtz, listened to the cricket and bird chirps that Carlson had recorded. After seeing the enhanced plant growth, Holtz said, *"It was thrilling to make that connection. I began to feel that God had created the birds for more than just freely flying about and warbling. Their very singing must somehow be intimately linked to the mysteries of seed germination and plant growth."*

Mohammed Azhar Khan, technical advisor to the Northwest Frontier Provinces' Farmers Association in Pakistan says, *"Using the Sonic Bloom sound frequencies and foliar sprays I have been able to increase potato yields by 150 percent over the national average and increase corn harvest by 85 percent over the national average."*

Herein lies the message that encouraging the birds and insects to sing in your garden will foster enhanced growth of your plants. I further feel, unscientifically, that chickens and other livestock behave better, are healthier, gain weight faster and produce more nutritious food if they hear the pre dawn bird sounds that abound in a healthy ecosystem. Who knows, maybe even the raucous, boisterous crowing of the rooster is a signal for plants to wake up and get growing!

It is important to remember that foliar feeding is not a substitute for healthy soil and generous applications of organic matter and fertilizers. Seaweed's largest value is in supplying minute quantities of trace elements in a readily usable form to plant and animal digestive systems. In animals, seaweed acts as a catalyst to enable the digestive tract to extract nutrients from the food supply. The same thing happens when we apply seaweed to the soil. It acts as a chelating agent to help plants glean minerals for an adequate diet.

A good rate of application for seaweed meal is 1 pound per 100 square feet, raked lightly into the soil. You can apply the seaweed directly to the soil in meal form, or you can supply it through the chicken's digestive tract. As we saw earlier, chickens utilize only about 20% of the mineral value of their feed, excreting the remainder. Fortunately, if the chicken manure goes directly to your garden soil you'll be able to recycle the amount of fertilizer contained in the manure.

When you are feeding seaweed meal in your chicken feed you will get back a portion of the seaweed meal in the manure. This amounts to about 1/3 of the total requirement for seaweed in your garden. Add the remainder by lightly broadcasting seaweed meal.

It is always difficult to measure the results of this kind of soil amendment. So many other factors play a role in total yields, such as weather, rainfall, organic matter in the soil, origin of fertilizer materials, varieties of plants, and so on. However, as a general rule, plan on a 10% increase in total yields when you apply seaweed meal to your garden.

In a 1,000 square foot garden, a good target is 1 pound yield per square foot of planted area. For mixed vegetable crops this is about $1 per square foot in crop value at retail pricing levels. If you can get a 10% increase in yields, it will be worth roughly $100 to you, yet only costs about $10 for the seaweed meal. That is a return on investment of 900%.

Permaculture Gardening

One way to measure soil health and productivity is by measuring the vegetable or fruit yields. The upper potential of a <u>healthy</u> soil production is at least 7 times greater than the current national average. We can grow at least 7 times more yields on rich, healthy soil than on poor soil.

If you use chicken tractors to improve your garden beds year after year, you can look forward to developing a fine rich soil that will eventually produce at least 7 times what it is producing now. Your first year garden will grow food for one family, but as you make your soil richer and improve your growing techniques you will experience a surplus of food. At that point you can begin decreasing your garden size each year, resulting in less and less work to get more and more food. Or, rather than decrease the garden size as it becomes more fertile, you can start selling the extra food to your friends and neighbors and create a market garden.

Once you start growing vegetables to sell, it is a simple matter to grow extra chickens to sell, too. However, there is an upper limit to the number of chickens you can grow in your backyard. At some point your little piece of land will become so rich that you just can't add any more chicken manure to it. So, as you add families to your marketing network you will need to add land for growing chickens.

At this point it is time to consider making yours a more holistic project by adding enough land to include grains in the crop rotations so that the chickens can fertilize the grain land as well. This will enable you to have enough chickens to feed 7 families, and not have to buy all the chicken feed.

Remember, as the land receives more organic matter it will grow richer and will need less irrigation water. The soil will be able to hold more of the natural rainfall that occurs. The idea is to make the garden soil structure such that it can soak up the rain fall. Then the soil acts as the reservoir for both nutrients and moisture. Mmmm, your plants will love it!.

Chapter 11: Marketing

Making an Income by Gardening with Happy Hens and Healthy Soil

The premise of this book is to show you how to grow your own great tasting poultry and eggs in a systematic method that will enrich your garden soil quickly and effectively. However, some of you will want to grow food for others.

It is entirely possible to start a small-scale part-time poultry business for less than $100. The profits you earn won't be large, but you will make enough money to make it worthwhile.

I first started doing this years ago when I got into a yearly cycle of buying and raising three feeder pigs. I planned on one pig for my own freezer and two to sell. The two that I sold each year brought in more than enough money to pay all the feed bills and the cost of the shelter. It takes just a tad longer each day to care for three pigs than for one, so my time wasn't a factor in whether I made a profit on the two pigs that I sold.

Now I do the same thing with chickens. I grow 120 chickens and keep 35 for my freezer. The 85 I sell bring in more than enough money to pay all the costs of my poultry operation. This is probably the "homestead" level of poultry production.

If you want to make some spending money from your efforts, just increase the size of your poultry project to the "Market Garden" level. With an initial investment of about $1,000 you can expect to earn a net income of about $3,000 in a typical 6-month season after you pay all expenses. This net income might be large enough to pay your house taxes or mortgage each year, or take you on a long awaited vacation if you want. The $3,000 income you earn can even be seed capital for expanding your business in the following year.

If you have $10,000 to $20,000 to invest you can even build a business where you can earn a respectable five figure full time income. Joel Salatin in Swoope, Virginia, is an example of this size business. With a $20,000 investment and 20 acres of land he and his wife earn over $25,000 net profit annually from their broiler business.

Practice Ensures Success

Every chicken grower that I know has more eggs or meat birds than they need for their own family, so they sell the extras. In most cases it's just enough income to help with the feed bills, but in some cases my friends do make quite a bit of money from their poultry project each year.

In the beginning, I'd like to encourage you to spend your first year practicing. Learn how to grow chickens for your own use. I think it's wise to do this for several reasons. First, you won't try to start too big. This is important because there is a learning curve in raising chickens just as there is in any other endeavor. Learn on your own time, make any mistakes quietly without anyone else relying on your performance. There will be plenty of time later to grow poultry for sale, either as a part-time or full-time endeavor.

If you don't have any experience in growing chickens for eggs or meat, you will need this first practice-year to get comfortable with the techniques. You will learn most of what you need to know about raising chickens from the first batch you grow. It is always comforting to start small and let your business grow slowly.

Growing chickens for your own use will give you the chance to find out several things. First, do you really like growing chickens, and do you want to do it as a business? Second, you will learn how wonderfully delicious these homegrown chickens are. If you know they are good to eat then you will be able to convince your potential customers. There's nothing like being sold on the product first to enable you to sell it easily to your family, friends and neighbors.

During the first season you will become much more familiar with all the costs and how much labor it takes. You will get a better idea of the land and buildings required for the business and you will gain the actual experience of producing your first batch of birds.

The average family will eat from one to two chickens per week. A 4 pound broiler will be enough to feed four hungry adults at dinner. Patricia and I eat 25 broilers per year, about 1 every other week. With just the two of us we generally get at least two meals out of each 4 pound bird. We also plan on an extra 10 birds per year for dinner parties and special occasions.

If we were to buy these 35 free range broilers from the store we would have to pay about $280. Since we grow them ourselves the real cost is about $175, not counting our labor. Besides, we don't really consider it labor, since it's one of our hobbies and we get a great deal of enjoyment out of it, along with super rich garden soil.

We always grow enough extra chickens to sell. This helps to pay all of our expenses and get our own freezer birds for free. If we grow an extra 85 broilers each year, and make $3 net profit per bird, we earn $255, more than enough to pay for the chickens we want for our own use each year.

You can grow 100 broilers per year using just one 4-foot by 10-foot chicken tractor. This requires 20 chickens per batch, and five batches per year. Raising five batches per year is fairly difficult in the colder climates, though. It makes more sense to use two chicken tractors, with 20 birds each, and raise 3 batches in one tractor and 2 batches in the other tractor. To make a little extra money, you can raise 120 broilers, with 20 per batch and 3 batches.

These 120 birds will pay all your overhead and operating expenses and pay for about 35 birds for your own use. You wind up with about $50 to $75 net profit. Please keep in mind that these cost figures are from my experience in my geographic area. I think the two big differences you might find in your area are the cost of feed and the cost of processing.

I pay $20.50 per hundredweight for certified organic chicken feed, yet I understand that other parts of the country have feed for as little as $7.50 per hundredweight. For processing, I have paid as high as $2.75 per bird if I want them vacuum packed in a freezer-duty plastic bag. Growers in other parts of the country are reporting as little as $1.50 per bird for processing. In some areas vacuum packing is not available.

I use the vacuum packing for two reasons. First, it makes a very presentable package for my customers. Second, I think it extends the freezer life and flavor of the bird. Because of these advantages I feel the extra cost of .65 or .75 cents per bird is okay.

You can see from the table below that your up front costs are just over $700 to start this small-scale business. At first glance this might seem like a large investment to make, but the return is very good, indeed. You will earn only $66 in cash, but you will have 40 chickens—worth $320—in your freezer. That's over 50 percent return on your investment, much better than a bank savings account or the stock market. The best part of this deal is your garden soil, which gets richer and richer each year.

Table 17: Sample Budget for a 120 Broiler Business.

Item	Cost
4 x 10 tractors (2)	$10 per year *
120 chicks	$60
Feed	$198 (1,800# x .11 cents #)
Brooder lamp	$2 per year *
Feeders/waterers	$4 per year *
Processing	$300 (120 x $2.50 each)
Total	$574
Income	$640 (80 x $8 each)
Net Profit	$66 plus 40 free broilers for your own use @ $8 each = $386
Total cash required:	$718 (includes up front costs of tractors, feed, equipment, chicks and processing.)

* Equipment has a useful life of 5 years, so I spread the cost over that period of time.

What if you don't <u>have</u> $718 to get started? Simple. Just presell your birds. Contact all your friends, family and neighbors and sell them on the idea of hiring you to grow their poultry for them. If you like the flavor and healthfulness of these homegrown chickens, then you can easily persuade your friends to buy from you. Share your budget with them as a way to encourage them to pay you up front.

This method of farm marketing, called Community Supported Agriculture (CSA), is becoming increasingly popular each year across the country. It's a simple marketing method in which the consumers pay the farmer to grow their food for them. It works equally well with poultry, beef, vegetables and just about anything else you can imagine, even orchard fruits.

Your new customers may not want to pay you all the money up front, but you don't need it all in advance anyway. In the beginning all you need is to buy materials to build the pens, buy the chicks and brooder equipment, and enough feed to last a couple of weeks. This means your customers can pay you in weekly or monthly installments. Spread the payments out any way you like, just so you have the money to spend when you need to buy more feed or pay for the processing.

Keep in mind too, that you are growing three different batches of birds, 40 to the batch, over a six month season. Since you have to buy the equipment and build the pens, initially, your first batch of 40 chickens will cost you $345. Then the second and third rotations will only cost $186 for each batch of 40 birds.

Now, what if you want to make a great deal more income per year by raising broilers for sale? Let's say you want to make $3,600 per year to pay the real estate taxes on your property, or part of your mortgage payment. You can earn this much by growing 1,200 birds to sell, if you can make a net profit of $3 per bird.

With this many birds to grow you might want to consider a different pen size. A 4-foot by 10-foot pen only holds 20 chickens. You'll be doing 3 batches of chickens of 400 each batch, so you will need 20 pens of this size.

However, you can build a 10- by 12-foot pen that will hold 80 birds at a time, so you only need 5 pens. Since 1,200 broilers per year requires more land than the typical garden, you will need access to a pasture or field of about 2 acres.

Keep in mind that you won't need all the $6,720 to start your first batch. Rather you will need enough money to buy the equipment and the first 400 chicks plus feed and processing costs. This totals $2,840. The second and third batches will each require only $1,940 up front cash.

I've added $100 per batch for hiring someone with a large truck or trailer to haul the birds to the processor. This many birds, 400 per batch, won't fit in a pickup truck. You can hire a local hauler with a livestock trailer, or you can rent a large U-Haul truck and put straw on the floor. If you use a U-Haul truck be sure to prop the door open for air to ventilate the chickens during transit.

It's important to look at these figures carefully before you decide to haul off and start a 1,200 broiler business. The most important figure of course, is the number of birds. Can you really sell that many in your area, easily? If the average family needs only 20 to 40 broilers per year, then you will need to find at least 30 to 60 households willing to pay that price and take that many.

What you will probably experience is some customers want only 5 or so, while others want fifty to a hundred. In my area there are many 1 and 2 person households. They buy smaller quantities than larger families do.

Not only do your customers have to be willing, they have to be able. This means they need to have the money available when you ask for it, and they need freezer space to handle the number of chickens they are buying from you.

Table 18: Sample Budget for a 1,200 Broiler Business

Item	Cost
Chicken tractors (5-10x10) @ $100 each	$100 (5 x $100 / 5 years) *
Chicks	$540 (.45 cents each)
Brooder lamps	$30 ($150 / 5 years) *
Feeders/Waterers	$50 ($250 / 5 years) *
Feed	$1,980 (18,000 x 11 cents per pound)
Hauling to processor	$300
Processing	$3,000
Total costs	$5,940
Income	$9,600
Net Income	$3,600
Cash Required up front	$6,720
Return on investment	53.6% not including your labor

* Equipment has a useful life of 5 years. Spread the cost over that number of years.

In the best of cases, your procedure will be to deliver the chickens to the processing house early in the morning. Then you pick up the processed birds in the late afternoon, and your customers come to your house that evening to pick them up from you.

There's quite a bit of phone calling involved in this, since you want your customers to come on time. Otherwise you will have left over birds to freeze to keep them from spoiling. Chicken spoils quicker than any other meat, sometimes within hours of processing, especially in really hot weather.

Nowadays, most families do not have a freezer, other than the small one in their refrigerator. This might mean you will have to provide freezer storage for your customers. You can either do this by buying large freezers, or you can rent freezer space at a nearby cold storage facility.

Most larger communities do have a cold storage facility. You can store your chickens there for several months and once each month you can withdraw enough to make deliveries to all your customers. Make sure you will be able to rent space there, and find out how much it will cost. Then add these costs to your total production figures. Also, be sure to calculate your cost of traveling to the facility every month and pulling out chickens for your customers to pick up. The time you spend doing this can add quite a bit to the cost of your broiler operation.

In my area the cost of storing frozen chickens in a cold storage facility is $15 per month per pallet. Each pallet holds about 150 chickens. This adds about 2 cents per pound to the cost for each month the chickens are in frozen storage. Then I add another 5 cents per pound to cover my time in going to get them and having them available for my customers to pick them up.

You might want to invest in several freezers if you have room for them in your basement, barn or garage. A large freezer that will hold 150 4-pound broilers will cost about $600, plus the electricity to run it. You might be able to buy one used for less money. Just be sure it is in good condition and dependable. You certainly don't want to lose a freezer full of broilers if the freezer stops working.

Here's How to Sell Your Chickens Before They Hatch

There's an old adage that says a "salesman" has a product and tries to get a customer to buy it, whereas a "marketer" has a customer and finds the product that the customer wants to buy. It's a big distinction, and one that will guide you to finding your customers before you grow the chickens. Wouldn't it be terrible to grow 1,200 broilers and not have anybody to buy them?

Before you even order the chicks you need to know how many you can sell. To be on the safe side you might even want to have deposits or even full payment for the number of birds your customers want. Interestingly, if you go out to your friends and neighbors with your business idea, and they don't buy from you, it's a really big reason not to start a poultry business. On the other hand, you might find such a strong demand for homegrown broilers that you can expand your crop and earn a larger income from it.

Two marketing words you might not be able to use in marketing your chicken tractor chickens are "organic" and "free range". To use the word "organic" means you raise you birds according to strict regulations and are inspected and certified by a recognized agency, otherwise you can't use the word in your advertising or packaging. Most likely you will not be able to use the term "free" range for your birds, because you grew them in portable pens rather than "free" range. I don't agree with the logic here. In the chicken tractor system the birds get a new patch of fresh grass to graze each day, which in my estimation is better for them then typical "free range" conditions. Check with your state department of agriculture for up-to-date regulations and interpretations.

The only real consumer protection against grower fraud is for the grower to know the consumer and vice versa. The most powerful word you can use to sell your chickens is "homegrown" and it's the one word the regulators can't take away from you. Use the phrase, "old fashioned flavor, homegrown goodness" and people will get the message.

How many birds can a grower sell without state or USDA approval? This varies all over the country. Two examples, Vermont and Pennsylvania have widely differing views.

Vermont growers can only sell 1,000 chickens locally each year without having them processed in a state inspected processing facility. If Vermont growers want to sell their chickens across the state line they need to have them processed at a USDA inspected facility. There is a federally inspected processing facility in Vermont but it doesn't do custom processing.

On the other hand, the state of Pennsylvania allows a grower to market up to 10,000 birds annually without being state or federally inspected. Pennsylvania is the 4th largest poultry producer in the country. You'd think there wouldn't be much room for a local grower to sell birds, but that's not true. One grower, Mike Yodar sells hundreds of chickens each year in the shadow of the big producers, and he gets $2.25 per pound when they are getting something like 65 cents per pound. You can do it too if you take the time to develop your market and find the people who value nutrition and taste above cost and convenience. Most people just pluck a chicken out of the cooler at the supermarket when they want one. You will need to do a bit of re-educating them, train them if you will.

Once you have practiced and learned the art and science of growing chickens for your own use, you are ready to learn how to market chickens to your friends, family and neighbors. I don't encourage anyone to try to sell homegrown poultry at wholesale. "At wholesale" means to sell poultry to restaurants, brokers, supermarkets; who then sell the product to customers at retail. The price you will be able to charge at wholesale is generally too low for you to cover all your expenses and make any profit.

Still, I don't want to discourage you from at least looking at the available wholesale markets in your area. Some growers have told me they can get wholesale prices as high as $1.75 per pound from their local specialty foods store or health food store.

One grower friend of mine, John Kleptz at LaPlatte River Angus Farm, regularly sells 1,000 broilers per year to the local IGA supermarket at $1.75 per pound. At that level he still makes $2 per bird, which he feels is more than enough to compensate him for his time and effort. The chickens are merely a sideline for his beef farm, and a hobby for John. The store marks the chickens up to $2.19 per pound, and they say the response is great. They always run out of John's chickens before they run out of buyers.

For the beginner though, I recommend you sell your chickens at retail to a select group of purchasers. You can easily find people who are willing to pay a fair price for your chickens. Just talk to all your friends and neighbors, spread the word that you have delicious homegrown poultry or eggs for sale, and you will get plenty of buyers.

How much you charge for your birds is entirely up to you, and your customers. If free range and organic broilers are selling in your area supermarkets for $2 per pound then that's what you should charge for yours. In some cases you can even charge more, depending on the market area that you are in.

However, I never advise charging more for your birds than the general market is willing to pay. First, if your price is too high you won't sell many birds. Second, when your price is too high your buyers will be continually looking for other suppliers who have homegrown birds and are selling them for more realistic prices.

In my area free range and organic birds are selling for $2 and $2.25 per pound respectively. At this price I can make about $3 per bird in profit. That's enough for me, my customers don't mind paying it, and I can sell all the birds I want to grow on a part time basis.

High prices per pound are what it takes to make the small-scale operation practical and feasible. However, a price that is too high will be counterproductive. High prices per pound are not sustainable in my view because the market is small and fickle. High priced vegetables and meats become available to only a limited few who have the money to pay the price.

On the other hand, you don't want to sell your birds too cheaply. They cost you money and time to grow and you want to earn a fair return for the effort.

Poor diet is a national problem and we won't solve it by raising prices unnecessarily and beyond the ability of people to pay. However, low prices have no better impact on diet because the farmers don't make enough money and either go out of business or government subsidies become necessary.

While I doubt if any of us will ever get rich by growing and selling birds in our backyard, I do feel that you can make a very satisfying hourly wage by doing it. For the hundred or so birds I raise and sell each year I make enough to continue the research on chicken tractors, along with getting my food for free.

Buy Local Because

When you go out to find a market for your birds use the "buy local because" marketing plan. This involves persuading your customers to buy from you because:

1. You are a local farmer, helping to keep productive land in use, and keeping their food buying dollars in the local economy.
2. You are maintaining and preserving open space in your community.
3. You are buying your chicken feed from local farmers, helping them keep their farms open and profitable.
4. You deliver your chickens the day you harvest them instead of days or weeks later like the supermarkets do.
5. You raise your chickens humanely, rather than in confined, battery cage systems.
6. Your birds have that homegrown goodness and old fashioned flavor that makes them delightful to cook and eat. They are lip smackin', finger lickin' good!
7. You are helping restore the environment by decreasing the pollution caused by factory raised birds and excessive transportation from out-of-state broiler factories.

Nationally, 250 million people consume 2.5 billion chickens per year. If we developed a cadre of small-scale growers, each producing 10,000 birds per farm per year we would need 250,000 broiler producers here in the United States. Compare that possibility with the 5 huge producers we currently have in this country.

With excellent tasting, healthy birds the consumption might increase, even double. This increased demand for poultry will provide small farm opportunities for yet another 250,000 producers. People could get out of the factories, find some marginal, inexpensive land, and go in the broiler business for less than $20,000 per farm, and make a good living at it.

Who Is Your Market?

Members of your extended family, your neighbors, associates at work, and general acquaintances are all good potential customers for your homegrown poultry. What I've found happening is that my original customers--primarily my friends—like these homegrown birds so much they brag about them to their friends, who then call me up to buy some. This is word-of-mouth advertising and is quite possibly the most powerful marketing tool available to you.

Get it started by hosting a dinner or cook-out and serve some of your homegrown finest. Then ask your dinner guests to be your marketing crew. Sure enough, they'll buy some and get their friends to buy some, too. Then, you're in business.

Sell Them Other Products, Too

If you are of a mind to, you can use your core group of broiler customers to help you expand your business. Get them to help you sell other products from your backyard market garden or small farm.

It may be that you are already selling vegetables or other products to your friends and neighbors. If so, you can expand your menu and sell many other things to this group. Examples are, eggs, laying pullets, turkeys, rabbits, geese, ducks, even pork and beef if you have enough land.

Once you've taken the time and gone to the effort of developing a core group or buyer's club, it will be a simple matter for you to expand the quantities and types of food you can grow for them. If you can grow most or all the fresh and stored food for these families, then you can increase your gross income per year to the $50,000 range. You can earn your full-time living from a very small piece of land. Then you will be doing what you really want to do, growing good food for good people.

Raising Pullets for Resale

Some of you may want to grow poultry, but not eat it. If you are in this category, then you can start growing pullets—young hens—for folks who want to have hens for eggs but don't want to bother with the time and effort to raise the young hens. A pullet is about 20 to 22 weeks old before she starts laying eggs. You can use these young hens for your soil fertility program, then sell them once they start laying. People who buy them from you will be able to use them to add fertility to their garden soil, and enjoy fresh eggs to boot.

A laying pullet sells for about $5. Unlike broilers, you don't have the expensive processing to pay for. If you can sell 100 pullets per year you will make a nice net income for yourself and get plenty of manure for your garden. You will also make it possible for a whole new group of families to become partially food self-sufficient by growing their own eggs.

Chapter 12: Processing Poultry

You have two choices, you can either slaughter the chickens yourself, or take them to a slaughter house in your area. Check with your local county extension office for slaughter houses in your part of the country. Sometimes they advertise in the local paper or you can ask around the feed stores and ask other growers for the names of local processing places.

Having the chickens slaughtered in a USDA inspected slaughterhouse will set you back anywhere from $2 to $3 per bird. There are two advantages of using an inspected facility. The inspector will tell you if your birds have any diseases, and you can legally sell your dressed poultry to the public.

I talked to Chuck DeCorley recently over at *Small Farm Today* magazine. He says his state, Missouri, has a real lack of processing houses. That surprises me. I grew up in southwestern Missouri at a time when every county had one or more slaughterhouses. Times have really changed, even in the conservative mid-west.

As I said earlier, you can probably make more money faster with a poultry processing business than you can as a poultry farmer. It may be that the laws in Missouri or other states make it prohibitively expensive to start a processing facility. If that's the case maybe you need to do some public activism to get the laws changed. It should be possible for any one to start a business, provided they have the capital and skills to do so.

If you do your own butchering it will help if you have proper equipment. Doing all the steps by hand can easily take one hour per bird, at least in the beginning. Even after you've had some practice you'll still be able to only do up to 4 birds per hour by hand.

With a killing cone, thermostatically controlled scalding vat and a table-top plucking machine you can undress a chicken in less than 5 minutes. This equipment will cost about $600 to $1,000 though. It will last you forever if you keep it clean and stored properly, and, quoting Gene Logsdon, "If you don't drive your truck over it".

One way to lower your individual cost for processing equipment is to joint venture with other small growers in your area. You can buy the equipment together and take turns using it. One of my grower buddies, John Kleptz did just that. He got so tired of paying the hefty processing fee that he bought his own slaughter house. Now he figures he makes more money processing other people's birds than he does growing his own. Actually, he may be right. As a grower I only make $2 to $3 per bird, and it takes 8 weeks to do it. He makes almost that much in 5 minutes, every time he processes someone else's broiler.

I think that building your own processing facility might not make economic sense unless you are processing thousands of birds each year. However, if you have the equipment, time and ability you can save $2 to $3 per bird by doing it yourself. There are several good guides available from your county extension agent for poultry processing.

Most of the small-scale growers I know take their broilers to their local processing plant. Sometimes it's easier for me to take them to the slaughterhouse the night before processing since it doesn't interfere with my work schedule. I think it also helps the flavor of the meat if the chickens get a chance to calm down after their ride in the truck. Excited chickens tend to build up lactic acid in their muscles. It's better to let them sit a few hours in their new surroundings before being processed.

John Adams, a local processor, tells me this delay in butchering helps the feathers come out easier during the plucking process. He also said it's easier to remove the entrails if you withhold feed for 12 hours before processing. Never withhold water, though. The chickens are apt to die on you.

I've done it both ways, and found that it is easier to harvest broilers at night rather than in the daytime. At night they are asleep. It's easy to pick them up and put them in the truck. When I harvest the chickens at night I put them in the truck with bedding and water, and plenty of ventilation. Then, I either drive them to the processing plant that evening or early next day. I can only carry up to 50 chickens at a time in my compact pickup truck. If I have more than that to haul I either rent a big U-Haul truck or hire a local livestock hauler who has a cattle trailer.

Some growers I've talked to use wooden chicken crates to move their broilers. These crates are expensive and hard to build, so I've always relied on either handling the chickens loose, or putting three at a time in used banana boxes. I get the boxes free from the dumpster behind the supermarket.

To catch chickens in the pen I use a large paddle made from a sheet of 1/4-inch plywood. This paddle traps them against one end of the pen where I can reach in and pull them out two at a time. I use the paddle to get the chickens out of the pickup truck cap too. Just stick it in through the window and nudge them back towards the tailgate where my helper can catch them and unload them.

Chapter 13: Raising Poultry Humanely

Chicken Tractor is the most humane, clean, sensible way to raise chickens and other poultry. The portable shelter-pens allow the birds plenty of exercise, sunshine and fresh air, while protecting them from the weather, predators and inhumane conditions. Using chicken tractor systems you can supply yourself and neighbors with wholesome humanely raised food while enhancing your garden.

We have included this article entitled "The Truth Behind A Hen's Life" because I have seen first hand how terrible the conditions are for chickens in the egg layer and broiler factories. I know there is a more humane and profitable way to raise wholesome, healthy meat birds and eggs. The way to do this is by raising them locally using more sustainable agricultural practices such as chicken tractors and pastured poultry. Also, as Dr. Adcock describes in the following article, "raising consumer awareness is one of the keys to a more humane world".

The Truth Behind "A Hens Life"

by Melanie Adcock, D.V.M.

Adapted and reprinted with permission from *Humane Society of the United States News*, Spring 1993

The hen is not unlovable or emotionless, but a thinking, sensitive and complex creature. A chicken can recognize and remember about 100 other chickens. Chickens enjoy playing with toys. Chickens like listening to classical music (Vivaldi in particular) while others cuddle up to red mittens for comfort. Knocking on the door before entering a small hen house will keep hens from being startled by a visitor.

When allowed to roam freely, hens are extremely active during the day—walking, running, flying, exploring and searching for food. At night they roost together, preferring to perch high off the ground.

Chickens are inquisitive animals and will closely investigate anything new in their environment. Hens like to work for their food. Even if food is readily available, hens choose to spend a large part of their day exploring for food and scratching and pecking at the ground.

Chickens are very social animals and form tight social groups. Groups of birds tend to dust-bathe (a grooming behavior) and eat together. They communicate with each other through visual displays and calls. The baby chick begins communicating while still inside the egg, responding to the mother's purring as she incubates the egg.

Nesting is extremely important to laying hens. They prefer to lay their eggs in a private nest, and they perform an elaborate sequence of behaviors while searching for a nest site, building the nest and laying eggs.

It is hard to imagine a less appropriate housing for the highly social complex and active laying hen than "battery" cages. These cages are made entirely of wire and are so small and cramped that hens cannot spread their wings. About 98 percent of all eggs sold in supermarkets come from hens who spend their entire productive lives—up to 2 years—crowded into tiny cages with other hens.

To limit the damage from the aberrant excessive pecking of cage mates in this restrictive barren environment, part of the hen's beak is removed, a practice termed "debeaking". A hen's beak is critical for preening, exploring, and feeding. Debeaked chickens show behavior changes suggesting short-term and long term pain. The severed nerve endings in the beak develop into abnormal nervous tissue, and the beak never heals properly.

A hen's nesting desire is so strong that she will go without food and water to be allowed to use a nest when she's ready to lay. Deprived of nests, hens in battery cages pace anxiously and repeatedly attempt to escape for hours prior to laying an egg. Without privacy or nests, they lay their eggs on the sloping wire floor where they are forced to stand. The birds are bred to be egg-laying machines, continuing to lay even when severely injured.

Hens suffer foot and feather damage from poorly designed wire cages unsuited to their needs. The wire floor doesn't allow dust-bathing, or scratching or pecking at the ground for food. The cramped quarters do not even permit normal preening or grooming. The complete lack of exercise coupled with the demands of high egg production causes bone weakness, predisposing the hens to broken bones. The first time they experience the out-doors is when they are sent to slaughter, often in open trucks.

You are the key and when you spend money at the grocery store you directly influence how food is made and how animals are raised. Every time you reach for a carton of eggs from battery caged hens, you are telling the grocer and egg industry that you accept that product and the current treatment of industry laying hens. Instead, for just pennies more, you can improve the lives of millions of laying hens by choosing cartons of eggs from humanely raised, uncaged hens.

Today, more humanely produced foods are not readily available in convenient locations such as local grocery stores. To confront this problem the Humane Society of the United States is mounting an "egg effort" in several major cities. They are joining forces with consumer, environmental, farmer and animal protection groups to bring eggs from uncaged hens into grocery stores and to urge consumers to support the more humane egg farmers.

The Humane Society's efforts to empower consumers to improve the lives of laying hens are part of a nationwide campaign asking consumers to "shop with compassion". Because the battery cage is one of the most inhumane systems for raising animals, it is the first target of their campaign. No other farm animal endures such extreme physical confinement and crowding for as long as the hen does. The Humane Society needs your help to spread the word about battery-caged hens and to urge all egg users to buy eggs from free-roaming hens.

To learn more about the Humane Societies "egg effort", contact:

The Humane Society of the United States
2100 L Street NW
Washington, DC. 20037
Phone (202) 425-1100, FAX (202) 778-6132

Chapter 14: Keeping Hens In The Chicken Tractor

You can use your chicken tractor in the garden during the day to let the chickens roam around searching for insects. Just install a pop hole on the end of the tractor to let them in and out. This works best in a maturing garden, of course. The chickens will eat a few leaves while they are looking for bugs, but probably less than the bugs themselves will eat.

This method works best if you let the chickens out in late afternoon. Most of them will have already laid their daily egg in the nest boxes by noon, so you don't have to hunt all over the garden to find any wayward eggs. As dusk begins the chickens will make their way back to the chicken tractor and you can go out in the evening and close their pop hole door.

One disadvantage of letting the chickens loose in the garden is they will come in contact with bird droppings from wild birds. Wild bird diseases may infect your chickens, but then the world is full of risks and you need to weigh the possible advantages with the disadvantages.

Egg layers need certain things that broilers don't, primarily a roost, a nest box and, in the winter, extra light.

1. Light, Egg Laying and Chicken Health

I think of light as a nutrient—just as important to the health of the chickens as vitamins. Light has a huge affect on all life, and it's particularly noticeable in chickens. The length of the day's light affects the egg laying cycle. In nature, when the days begin to shorten, the number of eggs they lay gradually decreases. Sometimes, egg laying will stop entirely in the wintertime. In the natural reproductive cycle, most poultry lay eggs in several batches when the light increases from spring to summer.

Figure 19: Light and Egg Production

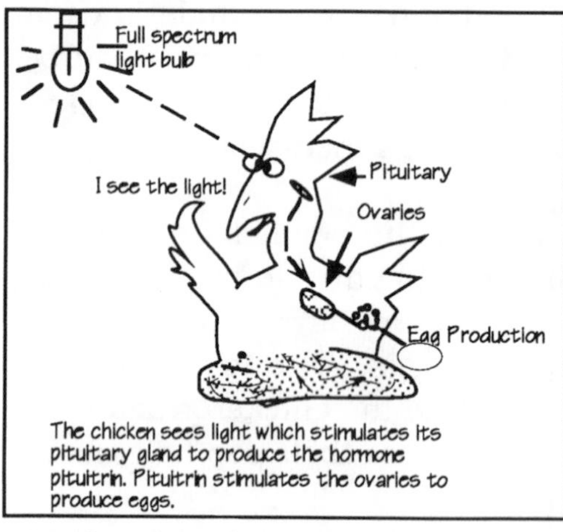

* Not drawn anywhere close to scale.

The domestic hen will produce eggs for a much longer time than her wild cousins. However, she will need supplemental light if she is to lay eggs during the shorter days of winter.

Measure light in intensity and length. The longest day of the year is the summer solstice in June, with daylight lasting about 17 hours. You might want to provide artificial light from July onwards through the Spring (Vernal) Equinox when the days are of equal length. This occurs around March 21 of every year.

Light intensity is the measure of light's brightness. Use a light meter to measure it in lux. A good level of light intensity for a hen house is about 10 lux, equivalent to natural sunlight

A dimmer is important to give the birds some warning that it will soon be dark. Chickens are just like us. They need time to find their perches and settle in for the night. If you don't have a dimmer, use a very low watt nightlight, so the birds can see to get on the roosts.

2. Roosts & Perches

Broilers don't need perches, but hens love them. It is essential to give them roosting space so they can live naturally. Their toes have evolved to allow them to lock around a perch so they can sleep without falling off.

A good perch is about 3 inches wide with a bevel of about 2 inches at the top. The bevel gives the roost a more natural structure for the chickens to grip. It also eliminates the sharp 90 degree angle that can be uncomfortable for the chickens. You can either use old wooden closet poles for perches or you can make them as shown in the following diagram. Don't use steel or aluminum pipe since the birds will have trouble gripping it.

Figure 19: Perch Dimensions

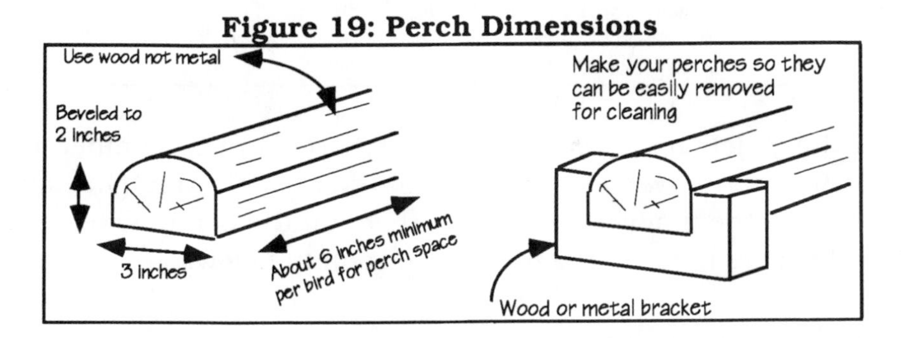

Perches need to be less than 2 feet from the ground. This is so the hens won't hurt their feet from continuous jumping down. Small cuts in the feet can result in infections and foot abscesses, commonly called bumblefoot.

Make multiple stepped perches about 16 inches apart. Allow a minimum roosting space of 6 inches per bird and preferably even more.

Figure 20: Multiple Perches

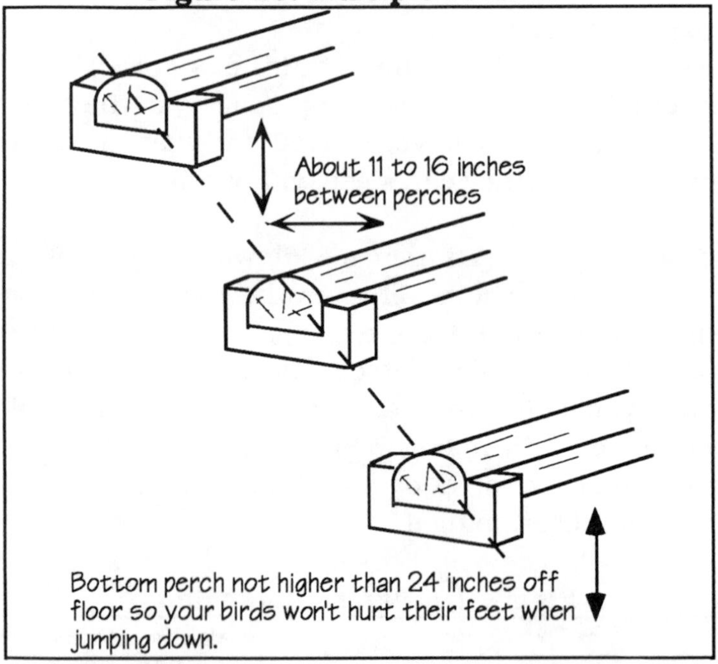

If the chickens or pullets you buy are from a commercial grower and have been in cages all their lives you might have to show them how to roost. Put them on the perch. Once one pullet gets the idea the others are soon to follow.

3. Pop-Holes (Chicken Doors)

Chickens need doors, too. A pop-hole is a chicken-sized door designed especially for the chickens to enter and exit their house. Build several pop-holes to open and close in a planned sequence to give access to the appropriate paddock(s).

With the use of a timer and solar panel, you can even have automatic opening and closing pop-holes such as the one on the Esalen Institute chicken house in Big Sur, California.

Figure 21: Pop-Holes (Chicken Doors)

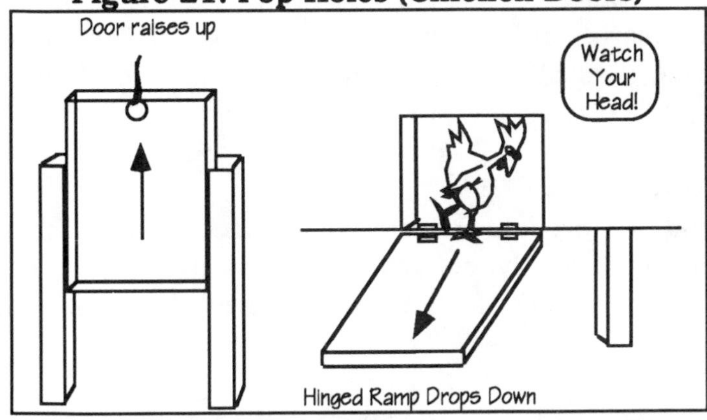

In paddocks that are muddy or wet, a ladder type ramp can also help the chickens to wipe their feet going in—much like a mud mat on your front door. The slots also allow the manure to fall to the ground instead of on the ramp where you would have to clean it. No, I've never seen a chicken intentionally wipe its feet before entering, but I know a fellow who taught his Black Lab Retriever to wipe her feet before jumping in the truck!

Figure 22: Raised Pop-hole with Ramp

For larger flocks you would want to put a larger pop-hole in so that several birds could enter and exit at the same time. Otherwise it could become "ambush pass" for chickens to harass each other.

4. Nesting Boxes

A nesting box provides a quiet, dark, secure place for hens to lay their eggs in privacy. Would you want to lay an egg with everybody looking? No, you would probably use a nesting box, too.

Usually, nesting boxes are about 12 inches high and deep and 10 inches wide. For larger hens you might need bigger boxes. A 3 inch strip along the bottom helps to keep the nesting material from falling out when the chicken leaves the box. One box for every 3 hens is a good ratio. When they are not nesting, they will be very comfortable on the roosts.

Having the nest dark helps prevent the hens from pecking and eating eggs. One way to make the nest darker is to put a curtain over the front of the box.

Figure 23: Static Nesting Box

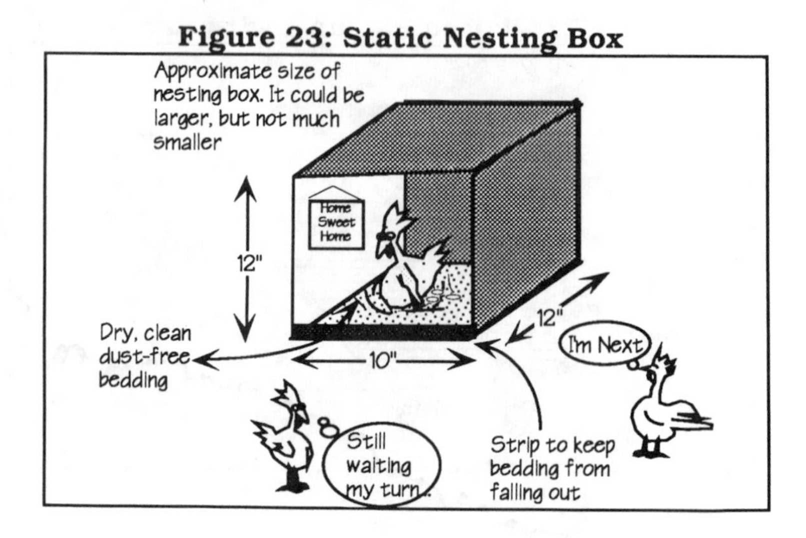

The threshold strip will allow the hens to enter and exit easily. This also helps the hens feel more secure and content while they are laying.

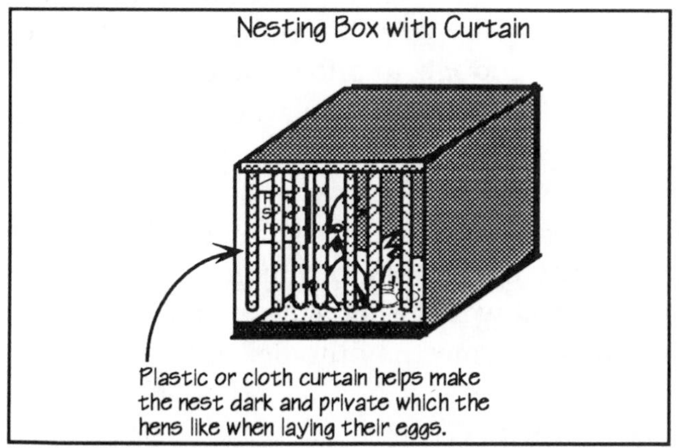

There are two types of nesting boxes—static and rollaway. The static box is level so eggs don't roll anywhere. The rollaway box, as its name implies, slants backwards so the eggs roll to the back for easier collection.

Figure 24: Roll-away Nest Box

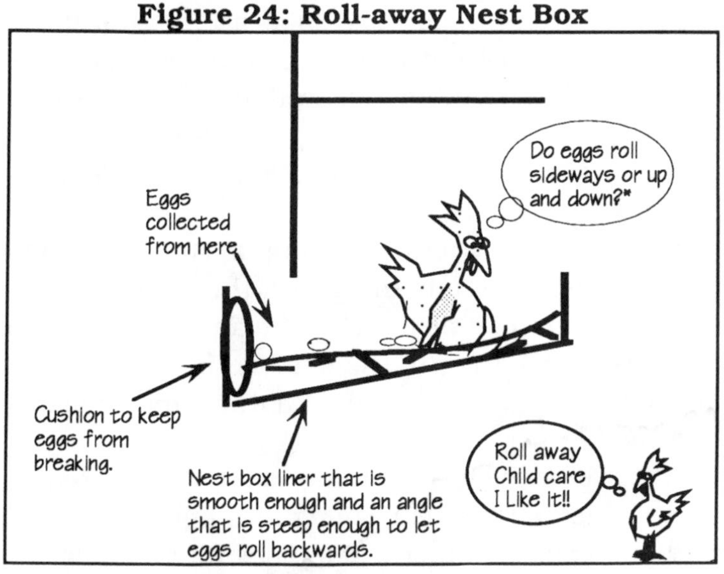

*Poultry riddle for Zen study.

I have not found the roll-away box to be practical for small hen houses or chicken tractors. By the time you get the angle steep enough for the eggs to roll backwards, the hens are on unlevel footing. Additionally, the nest box bedding must be smooth enough to allow the eggs to roll. I prefer the natural bedding of straw, hay or wood chips. These materials would not help win an egg race to anywhere.

It is much more convenient to have access to nest boxes from outside the egg mobile or chicken tractor. I can do this by using a hinged waterproof access door that opens directly to the nesting box from the outside.

5. Nesting Materials

You can use anything that is relatively clean, dry and dust free as nesting material. Sawdust tends to be too fine and dusty. You can use wood shavings, but never from pressure treated lumber because of the risk of arsenic poisoning.

Chopped straw or hay is very good as long as it is free of harvest mites. Also keep it dry so that mold doesn't form. The spores from the mold *Aspergillus fumigatus* can cause congestion and wheezing, symptomatic of aspergillosis. "Farmer's lung" is a common name for this disease.

There are also synthetic nesting materials, some that resemble grass. The advantage of these is that you can remove them for cleaning. The advantage to the natural materials is you can put them in your compost pile and enrich your soil. I prefer to use all natural materials.

You want to remove eggs from the nesting area frequently so that they do not get broken. Sometimes hens learn to peck at the eggs—especially broken ones. They like the egg shell as a source of calcium.

Chapter 15: Other Animal Tractors

With only slight variations you can adapt the chicken tractor idea to other types of livestock, including quail, pheasants, turkeys, ducks, geese, guinea, rabbits, pigs and, in a big enough pen, beef.

Some of the changes you might want to make are to build larger pens for larger fowl such as turkeys, or add netting to keep wild flying birds such as pheasants from escaping when you open the lid to feed and water them.

Table 18: Turkey Breeds From Commercial Breeders

Broad breasted Bronze	Stately, large up to 38 pounds, hens to 22 pounds, feathers sheen copper to bronze to burnished gold, six foot wing span
Giant White	Popular broad breasted turkey, hens to 25 pounds and toms to 45 pounds
Bourbon Red Turkeys	Beautiful, medium size, slower to mature, good to eat
Wild Turkeys	Hardy and colorful, good flyers, very tasty, for table or game birds. Check wildlife regulations in your area, you may need a permit to raise these wild turkeys, even for table use, and you may not be able to raise them for market sales.

Excerpted with permission from Murray McMurray Hatchery catalog

According to the American Livestock Breeds Conservancy, Bronze Unimproved and many other strains of turkeys are available without the broad-breasted gene. Because they are standard breeds you can breed them on the homestead.

Table 19: Ducks, Geese, Pheasants, Partridge, Guineas.

White Pekin	China, fine meat quality and egg laying, creamy white, large breasted, easy to pick and prepare, males 10-11 pounds, females 8-9 pounds
Rouen	France, similar to wild Mallard, males to 8-9 pounds, females to 6-7 pounds.
Cayuga	New York, Lake Cayuga, brilliant "beetle" green plumage. Hens to 5-6 pounds, lay blue-gray eggs, males to 6-7 pounds
Flying Mallard	Smaller, with gamey flavor
Khaki Campbell	General purpose, good layers, mature at 4.5 pounds, easy to pick for table use, excellent foragers and hardy
Fawn and White Runners	Scotland, small, good foragers, white eggs
Buff Ducks	England, good layers, not broody, hens up to 7 pounds and drakes up to 8 pounds
Blue Swedish	Very hardy, good foragers, up to 8 pounds, mostly white eggs some blue or gray tinted
Goslings	
Toulouse	France, all-dark meat, males 18 to 20 pounds and females 12 to 13 pounds
White Embden	Germany, pure white, easy to dress, great taste, males 20 pounds, females to 13 pounds, showy as purebreds
White Chinese	Very hardy, good layers, good hatch, showy and make good watch dogs
Weeder Geese	China, they love weeds but not fruits of garden plants, great foragers and garden companions

Pheasants	
Red Golden	Beautiful, China, hardy, easy to raise, valued feathers, slow to mature
Buff Pheasant	Used for stocking hunting clubs
Lady Amherst's Pheasants	China, very pretty, easy to raise and prized for feathers, slow to mature
Black-Necked Pheasant	Western Europe, coppery red with dark head and neck and brown shoulders
Afghan Pheasant	Small, alert, quick and good flyers, likes arid climate
Silver Pheasant	Southern China, easy to raise and breed
Reeves Pheasant	China, long-tailed, fast grower in first year
Chinese Ringneck Pheasant	China, beautiful, delicious, will grow wild
White Pheasants	Jumbo size, easy to raise and clean, delicacy
Jumbo Ringneck Pheasants	Larger than Chinese Ringnecks, raised for meat production, taxidermy and ornamental
Chukar Partridge	You may need a permit, can be domesticated or wild, a real treat for the table
Guineas	All-dark, gamey tasting meat, easy to raise, live on bugs, insects and weed seeds, very active foragers will eat deer ticks, acts as watch dog
Purple Guineas	Dark black with purple sheen
Coral Blue Guineas	Polka dots, very appealing
Lavender Guineas	Very striking color pattern
Slate Guineas	Very rare in U.S.
Buff Dundotte and Buff Guineas	Soft buff color with polka dots on Dundotte and no dots on Buff
White and Pearl Guineas	White's have albino plumage and skin, Pearl's are most common guineas with purplish-gray plumage "pearled"

Excerpted with permission from Murray McMurray Hatchery catalog

Appendix

Recommended Books for Small-Scale Agriculturists

The following books are available from your local bookstore or from the individual publishers. If you are unable to locate them in your area contact Good Earth Publications, P. O. Box 898, Shelburne, Vermont, 05482, phone and fax 802-425-3201.
Prices do not include shipping and handling.

Backyard Market Gardening, The Entrepreneur's Guide To Selling What You Grow, Andy Lee, 1993, Good Earth Publications, Shelburne, Vermont, 351 pp., $25

The Contrary Farmer, Gene Logsdon, Chelsea Green Publishing, Post Mills, Vt., 1993, 237 p. hard cover, $22

Sell What You Sow, Eric Gibson, 1993, New World Publishing, Carmichael, California, 302 pp., $23

Raising Poultry Successfully, Will Graves, Williamson Publishing, Charlotte, Vermont, 192 pp., $10

Raising Poultry The Modern Way, Leonard Mercia, 1990, Garden Way Publishing, Pownal Vermont, 234 pp., $10

Your Chickens, A Kid's Guide To Raising and Showing, Gail Damerow, Storey Comm. Inc., Pownal, VT, 156 pp., $13

Backyard Livestock, George P. Looby, The Countryman Press, Woodstock, VT., 225 pp., $15

The CHICKEN HEALTH Handbood, Gail Damerow, 1994, Storey Communications, Pownal, Vermont

Garden of Microbial Delights, Dorian Sagan and Lynn Margulis, 1988, 231 page hardcover, HBJ,Boston, MA., $25

Start With The Soil, Grace Gershuney, 1993, Rodale Press, Emmaus, PA., 275 page hardcover, $25

The Rodale Book of Composting, new revised addition, Rodale Press, Emmaus, PA., 278 pp., $15

Introduction To Permaculture, Bill Mollison, 1991, Tagari Publications, Australia, 198 pp., $25

Permaculture; A Designer's Manual, Bill Mollison, 1990, Tagari Publications, Australia, 576 pages, hard cover, $45

The Permaculture Book of Ferment and Human Nutrition, Bill Mollison, Tagari Publications, Australia, 288 pp., $27

Living Community, A Permaculture Case Study at Sol y Sombra, Ben Haggard, Center for the Study of Community, Santa Fe, New Mexico, 152 pp., $15

The Permaculture Way, Practical Steps To Create A Sustainable World, Graham Bell, 1992, Thorsons Harper Collins, NY, 240 pp., $16

Secrets of the Soil, Christopher Bird and Peter Thompkin

The Ecology of Commerce, A Declaration of Sustainability, Paul Hawken, Harper Collins, NY, 250 p. hard cover, $23

Pastured Poultry Profit$, Net $25,000 in 6 months on 20 acres, Joel Salatin, Polyface Inc., Swoope, Va., 330 pp., $30, companion video, one-hour, $50

Your Money or Your Life, Transforming Your Relationship With Money and Achieving Financial Independence, Joe Dominguez and Vicki Robin, Penguin, NY, 350 pp., $12

Beyond The Limits, Confronting Global Collapse, Envisioning a Sustainable Future, Donella Meadows, Chelsea Green Publishing, Post Mills, Vermont, 300 pp., $15

Holistic Resource Management, Allan Savory, Island Press, Covelo, California, 564 pp., $27

Greener Pastures On Your Side Of The Fence, Better Farming with Voisin Grazing Management, Bill Murphy, Arriba Publishing, Colchester, Vermont, 298 pp., $20

Farming In Nature's Image, an Ecological Approach to Agriculture, Judith Soule and Jon Piper, Island Press, Covelo, California, 286 pp., $20

How To Grow More Vegetables Than You Ever Thought Possible on Less Land Than You Can Imagine, John Jeavons, Ten Speed Press, Berkeley, California, 175 pp., $15

The New Organic Grower, A Master's Manual of Tools and Techniques for the Home and Market Gardener, Eliot Coleman, Chelsea Green Publishing, Post Mills, Vermont, 268 pp., $20

The New Organic Grower's Four Season Harvest, How to harvest fresh, organic vegetables from your home garden all year long, Eliot Coleman, Chelsea Green Publishing, Post Mills, Vermont, 206 pp., $18

Taking Stock: The North American Livestock Survey, and *The American Minor Breeds Handbook,* both from the American Livestock Breeds Conservancy, $15 and $8 respectively.

Resource Guide

Chick Producers and Equipment Dealers
Abendroth Hatchery, Rick Abendroth
W8697 Island Road, Waterloo, WI 53594
Phone 414-478-2053, Fax 414-478-2004

Clearview Hatchery
Box 399, Gratz, PA., 17030, Ph.717-365-3234, fax 365-3594

FarmTek
RR2 Box 17
Hopkinton IA 52237, 1-800-895-1598
Poultry growing equipment

Holderreads' Waterfowl Farm and Preservation Center
P. O. Box 492, Corvallis, Oregon 97339, Phone 503-929-5338

Johnny's Selected Seeds
Foss Hill Road
Albion, Maine 04910-9731, 207-437-4301
Cover crop seeds, vegetable seeds, books, tools, good advice

Kuhl Plastic Poultry Equipment
P. O. Box 26 Kuhl Road
Flemington, N.J. 08822, phone 908-782-5696

Marti Poultry Farm
P. O. Box 27, Windsor, MO 65360-0027, Ph. 816-647-3156

Mellinger's Inc.
2310 West South Range Road,

North Lima, OH 44452-9731, 800-321-7444, rooted comfrey cuttings, major greenhouse and garden supplier

Moyer's Chicks
266 East Paletown Road
Quakertown, PA 18951, Ph. 215-536-3155

Murray McMurray Hatchery
Webster City, Iowa 50595-0458
Order: 1-800-456-3280, FAX: 515-832-2213

Necessary Trading Company
One Nature's Way, New Castle, VA 24127, 703-864-5186
Feed supplements, kelp, diatomaceous earth, books, tools, good advice

G.Q.F. MFG. Co.
P. O. Box 1552
Savannah, GA 31498-2701
Poultry and Game Breeders Catalog

Well-Sweep Herb Farm
317 Mt. Bethel Road
Port Murray, NJ 07865, rooted comfrey cuttings, free catalog

Wild Acres,
HC83, Box 108
Pequot Lakes, MN 56472, Phone 218-568-5748 or 568-5024

Magazines and publications
Appropriate Technology Transfer For Rural Areas (ATTRA)
P. O. Box 3657
Fayetteville, Arkansas 72702, 1-800-346-9140, free publications on small-scale farming topics

Countryside and Small Stock Journal
N2601 Winter Sports Rd.
Withee, WI 54498 715-785-7979

Maine Organic Farmer and Gardener
RR 2, Box 594, Lincolnville, ME 04849

National Poultry News
P. O. Box 1647
Easley, SC 29641, 803-855-0140

Natural Farmer
Northeast Organic Farmers Association
411 Sheldon Rd., Barre, MA 01005, phone 508-355-2853

The New Farm
Rodale Institute
222 Main St.
Emmaus, PA 18098, 610-967-8405

NOFA NOTES
Vermont Northeast Organic Farmers Association
P. O. Box 697, Richmond, VT 05477

Organic Gardening
Rodale Press
33 E. Minor Street
Emmaus, PA 18098 215-967-5171

Permaculture Activist
Route 1, Box 38
Primm Springs, TN 38476

Permaculture Drylands Journal
P. O. Box 133
Pearce, Arizona 85625, 602-824-3465, fax 824-3542

Rural Heritage
281 Dean Ridge Lane
Gainesboro, TN 38562-5039, Phone and Fax 615-268-0655

Small Farm Today
3903 W. Ridge Trail Rd.,
Clark, MO 65243, Ph. 800-633-2535

Small-Scale Agriculture
Office of Small-Scale Agriculture, USDA/CSRS
Howard "Bud" Kerr, Director
Ag Box 2244
Washington, DC 20250-2244, Free quarterly publication

Associations to Join

The American Livestock Breeds Conservancy
Box 477, Pittsboro, North Carolina 27312, Ph. 919-542-5704

American Poultry Association Inc.
26363 S. Tucker Rd., Estacada, OR 97023

The Humane Society of the United States
2100 L Street, NW, Washington, DC 20037
Phone 202-452-1100, Fax 202-778-6132

National Contract Poultry Growers Association
P. O. Box 824, Ruston, LA 71273, 1-800-259-8100

Bibliography

Fryer, Lee, *The Bio-Gardener's Bible,* Chilton Book Company, Radnor, Pennsylvania,1982.

Damerow, Gail, *Your Chickens: A Kid's Guide to Raising and Showing*, Storey Communications, Inc. Pownal, Vermont, 1993

Fryer, Lee, *The New Organic Manifesto,* Earth Foods Associates, Inc., Wheaton, Maryland, 1986

Gershuney, Grace and Smillie, Joseph, *The Soul of Soil,* Gaia Services, St. Johnsbury, Vermont, 1986

Harris, Ben Charles, *Comfrey, What You Need To Know*, Keats Publishing, New Canaan, Connecticut, 1982

Holderread, Dave, *Raising the Home Duck Flock*, Storey Communications, Inc. Pownal, Vermont, 1978

Jeavons, John, *How To Grow More Vegetables**, Ten Speed Press, Berkley, California, revised 1991

Mercia, Leonard S. *Raising Poultry the Modern Way*, Storey Communications, Inc. Pownal, Vermont, 1990

Mollison, Bill, *Permaculture; A Practical Guide for a Sustainable Future,* Island Press, Washington, D.C., 1990

Mollison, Bill, and Slay, Reny Mia, *Introduction To Permaculture,* Tagari Publications, Tyalgum, NSW, Australia, 1991

Organic Gardening Staff, *The Encyclopedia of Organic Gardening*, Rodale Press, Emmaus, Pennsylvania, 1978

Salatin, Joel, *Pastured Poultry Profit$* Polyface Inc., Swoope, Va. 1994

Stockman Grass Farmer, *Alternative Marketing*, audio tape, Grass Farmer Library, Jackson, MS., 1990

Thear, Katie, *Free-range Poultry*, Farming Press Books, 4 Friars Courtyard, Ipswich, UK, 1990

Tompkins, Peter and Bird, Christopher, *Secrets of the Soil*, Harper and Row, New York, 1989

Index

A

B

C

M

N

O

P